ORTHO'S *All About*

Greenhouses

Meredith® Books
Des Moines, Iowa

Ortho® Books
An imprint of Meredith® Books

All About Greenhouses
Editor: Michael McKinley
Building Editor: Kenneth Sidey
Contributing Editor: Nellie Neal
Contributing Technical Editors: John W. Bartok, Jr.,
    Janice Hale, Martin Miller, Felder Rushing, Charles S.
    Yaw
Contributing Writers: Larry Hodgson, T. Jeff Williams
Art Director: Tom Wegner
Assistant Art Director: Harijs Priekulis
Copy Chief: Terri Fredrickson
Managers, Book Production: Pam Kvitne,
    Marjorie J. Schenkelberg
Contributing Copy Editor: Barbara Feller-Roth
Contributing Technical Proofreader: Fran Gardner
Contributing Proofreaders: Mary Duerson, Tamara Rood,
    Barbara J. Stokes
Contributing Map Illustrator: Jana Fothergill
Indexer: Ellen Davenport
Electronic Production Coordinator: Paula Forest
Editorial and Design Assistants: Kathleen Stevens,
    Karen Schirm

Additional Editorial Contributions from
    Art Rep Services
Director: Chip Nadeau
Designers: lk Design
Illustrators: Shawn Wallace

Meredith® Books
Editor in Chief: James D. Blume
Design Director: Matt Strelecki
Managing Editor: Gregory H. Kayko
Executive Ortho Editor: Larry Erickson

Director, Retail Sales and Marketing: Terry Unsworth
Director, Sales, Special Markets: Rita McMullen
Director, Sales, Premiums: Michael A. Peterson
Director, Sales, Retail: Tom Wierzbicki
Director, Book Marketing: Brad Elmitt
Director, Operations: George A. Susral
Director, Production: Douglas M. Johnston

Vice President, General Manager: Jamie L. Martin

Meredith Publishing Group
President, Publishing Group: Stephen M. Lacy
Vice President, Finance and Administration: Max Runciman

Meredith Corporation
Chairman and Chief Executive Officer: William T. Kerr

Chairman of the Executive Committee: E.T. Meredith III

Thanks to
Spectrum Communication Services, Inc., Elizabeth Neils,
    Charley's Greenhouses & Garden Supplies, and
    Gardener's Supply Company

Photographers
(Photographers credited may retain copyright ©
    to the listed photographs.)
L = Left, R = Right, C = Center, B = Bottom, T = Top
William Adams: 11CR, 25, 43; **Max E. Badgley:** 72T;
John Bartok/Univ. of Conn: 11TLC, 11CBL, 11TR, 26B,
29, 31, 35, 37, 45, 55, 57C, 59, 63; **John Blaustein:** 3T, 4,
12; **Ralph S. Byther:** 73B; **Kristi Callan:** 69TC, 71T, 74;
James S. Coartney: 72B; **Alan Copeland:** 22T; **Gardener's
Supply Co.:** 53; **Charley's Greenhouses & Garden
Supplies:** 24B, 52; **Crandall and Crandall:** 8; **Derek Fell:**
81, 84L, 87B, 88R; **John Glover:** 9T, 28B, 65B, 68B, 77L;
David Goldberg: 78, 79, 86L, 87T, 89B, 90T; **Doug
Hetherington:** 18, 22TC, 22BC, 22B, 23; **Saxon Holt:** 5,
11TRC, 11CBR, 26T, 28T, 39, 47, 54, 57B, 58;
Horticultural Photography: 9B; **Jerry Howard/Postive
Images:** 11BL, 49, 62, 76, 88L; **Tony Howarth:** 11TL, 33;
Michael Landis: 21, 82, 83; **Andrew Lawson:** 86R, 91B;
Janet Loughrey: 13; **Fred Lyon:** 89T; **Robert E. Lyons:**
71B; **Wayne S. Moore:** 69BC; **Ortho Photo Library:** 11CL,
11BR, 20, 27T, 41, 51, 65T, 67; **C.C. Powell:** 73T; **Robert
D. Raabe:** 70B; **Karen S. Rantzman:** 77R; **Julie Maris
Semel:** 3B, 64; **Richard Shiell:** 91T; **Betsy Strauch:** 85B;
Joseph G. Strauch, Jr.: 85T; **Steve Struse:** 66; **Dan Stultz:**
19; **Lauren Bonar Swezey:** 69B, 70T; **Univ. of IL-Urbana:**
69T; **Rick Wetherbee:** 24T, 57T, 60, 61, 68T, 75, 80, 84R,
90B

On the cover: Photograph by Janet Loughrey

All of us at Ortho® Books are dedicated to providing you
with the information and ideas you need to enhance your
home and garden. We welcome your comments and
suggestions about this book. Write to us at:
    Meredith Corporation
    Ortho Books
    1716 Locust St.
    Des Moines, IA 50309–3023

If you would like more information on other Ortho
products, call 800-225-2883 or visit us online at
www.ortho.com

CHOOSING THE RIGHT GREENHOUSE

Warm and welcoming, this elegant glass greenhouse glows with night lighting. You can tend plants after work, or just enjoy a cup of tea as you admire them, with the backdoor and garden a few steps away.

One glimpse into a garden with a greenhouse and you know there's a devoted gardener nearby. Just the sight of the covered structure sparks curiosity about what's growing inside: seedlings for this year's garden or treasured plant collections, maybe a combination of gift orchids and newly rooted perennials. You know you can talk plants here, and perhaps come away with a cutting or two simply for the asking.

When you decide to build a greenhouse, you give in to the gardener's fondest desire: to grow plants year-round. You can create a haven for tender plants, and at the same time provide a personal retreat. The warmth and humidity, the green surroundings, and the distinct rhythm of caring for plants in a greenhouse run pleasantly counter to the stresses of the world outside. Having your own greenhouse means there's no end to your personal gardening growth, either, because

benches, paths, and much equipment can readily be modified to suit changing needs.

Because you control the environment, virtually no plant is beyond your reach. The greenhouse offers protection and space for seeds that need bottom heat to sprout, cuttings that root only with high humidity, and blooming plants that need maximum light. Traditional gardening seasons do not apply; tropicals grow nonstop, flowers for cutting bloom all year, herbs and tomatoes know no limits.

Each gardener finds personal pleasures in the greenhouse. It can be a solitary escape where hours pass like minutes, or a place to set up a couple of chairs, plug in the coffeepot, and welcome friends for potting and conversation.

Whether it holds rare succulents or a bench full of blooming bulbs destined for lucky friends, a greenhouse pays big dividends. Caution to the passionate person who builds one: You may find yourself drawn to other serious gardeners. You'll find societies and specialty nurseries for the plants you love. Vacation plans will include the beautiful public greenhouses across the world. All that will inspire you to grow even more. And you'll be able to, with the help you find in this book.

USING THIS BOOK TO PLAN YOUR GREENHOUSE

Your greenhouse will be a practical structure well suited to your needs if you think the project through before buying anything. Think first about how you intend to use the greenhouse. Making a place to start seeds once a year is a much simpler project than designing a greenhouse for a wide selection of palms. The decisions you make now will guide you in choosing a site, the best kind and style of structure for your needs and budget, and its size, covering, and equipment. Planning begins with a consideration of greenhouse plans and kits, and the construction challenges and operating costs of each type. To proceed confidently, you must weigh the challenges of building it yourself or working with a contractor, and resolve any local tax, permit, and code issues.

USING THIS BOOK TO BUILD AND MANAGE THE STRUCTURE

This book begins with an explanation of how a greenhouse works and where to locate one to make the most of your site and conditions. That knowledge will help you decide whether to build from scratch or begin with a kit, and answer questions of style and materials. Use this book to walk through each phase of greenhouse building, from construction basics and equipment options to plans for 10 greenhouses. The plans described in this book require a variety of skill levels and represent a range of costs. Each greenhouse plan offers tried-and-true techniques you can depend on and refer to as you build.

Each major component of a greenhouse—from ground to roof's peak, benches, and growing areas—receives detailed attention. A range of equipment is discussed for moderating temperature, managing light, and providing water and fertilizer. This book offers information about manual and automated systems as well as solar options.

You'll use the last two chapters to schedule planting and greenhouse maintenance projects, and learn more about favorite plants. Explore the cultural information to anticipate and solve common problems in both growing and management. Refer to the calendar on pages 76 and 77 to know what maintenance

This orchid collector's greenhouse uses benches, islands, shelves, and hangers to make the most of a small space.

tasks to do and how to keep them on schedule for good greenhouse health. Use it to remind yourself of fertilizer regimes and seasonal needs for added lighting or shade, and how to prevent pest problems with timely cultural practices. Details about plant groups will make their care easier, and a year's worth of projects will inspire you to use the greenhouse in every season.

ASSESSING YOUR NEEDS

Consider the following questions when choosing a greenhouse.

■ How big a greenhouse do you need? Generally, at least 100 square feet is necessary to allow for benches and aisles. Most experts recommend making it larger than you think you need, because you will probably want to add more benches. In many cases, available space will restrict the size.

■ What is your purpose in having a greenhouse? If your goal is to raise vegetables and flowers the year around, a warm greenhouse with maximum light and headroom may be necessary. Your greenhouse could have less light and headroom if all you want to do is grow houseplants. If you require only a space to start plants from seed, you may be satisfied with a small, temporary greenhouse covered with plastic film.

■ What is your time commitment? A greenhouse takes time to run and maintain. It does little good to plan for an elaborate greenhouse and end up letting it sit idle because you couldn't find the time to keep it going. Be realistic about the amount of time you have.

■ Is a building permit necessary? Are there local design or zoning ordinances? Must the structure be set back a certain distance from property lines? Whether you are assembling a prefabricated kit or constructing your own structure from a plan, you will probably need a building permit. Also, you will probably need to adhere to certain construction specifications as well as design and setback ordinances. Consult your local building department or planning board at the outset.

■ Does a greenhouse mean higher property taxes? That may depend on how taxes are levied locally and whether your greenhouse is classified as permanent or temporary. Check with the assessor.

■ How much does it cost to supply a greenhouse with heat, water, and electricity? Depending on where you live, the heating cost can be very high and may dictate the size, shape, and construction of your greenhouse. Your utility company can help estimate the cost of heating different types of greenhouses. You may also consider solar heating (see page 27).

■ What does your budget permit? Materials for the hoop greenhouse shown on page 32 may be as inexpensive as $200, whereas a prefabricated glazed kit of similar size may cost as much as $10,000.

HOW A GREENHOUSE WORKS

Shade cloth can help protect plants from excessive sunlight in summer.

Fans help circulate and cool the air, exchange gases, and control humidity.

Ridgeline vents permit excess heat and humidity to escape.

Greenhouse coverings of glass, polycarbonate, acrylic, fiberglass, and plastic film admit sunlight to varying degrees.

Sturdy frames can be built from wood or extruded metal.

Benches, ground-level growing beds, shelves, and hangers provide growing areas at different heights to maximize space and light.

Sidewalls can be glazed to the ground, or framed and insulated below the level of the growing area.

A misting system is useful for increasing humidity in arid climates. Watering plants and using humidifiers and evaporative cooling systems can also increase humidity.

Windows, roof vents, louvered vents, and even the greenhouse door provide fresh air, usually pulled through the greenhouse by an exhaust fan at the same level on the opposite wall.

Supplemental heat can come from natural gas, electric, propane, or kerosene heaters, or from passive solar collectors. Shown here is a gas heater.

Utility hookups provide electricity, water, and gas to run greenhouse equipment. Install according to local codes before building a foundation; the water line should be trenched below the frost line for your area.

Whether you build your own greenhouse or buy a kit, you'll need to install a sturdy foundation for support.

Flooring materials range from a poured concrete pad or a paved walkway to gravel, bark chips, or even bare earth.

A greenhouse collects sunlight, which heats the air and elevates humidity around plants. Venting releases heat and exchanges carbon dioxide and oxygen. Water and fertilizer provide plants with the energy they need to continue growing. Your goal as you tend the greenhouse is to keep the conditions within the ranges preferred by your plants.

A greenhouse is a sunny area that is covered with clear materials designed to transmit light into the growing space inside. The sun is the primary heat source for the structure, but most greenhouses require additional heat.

Watering plants and walkways increases the humidity in the environment to enhance growing conditions; misting systems, humidifiers, and evaporative coolers also increase humidity. Because the plants grow actively, and both heat and humidity build up, ventilation and fans become necessary to exchange gases, cool and circulate the air, and reduce the spalike atmosphere in the house.

Plants thrive when light, moisture, heat, humidity, and fertilizer are available in optimum amounts. Whatever their specific needs, all plants get energy to grow from the carbon dioxide and water they absorb through leaves and roots. They use these molecules in the presence of light to produce sugar, the essence of their growing energy. In the process, they give off oxygen, heat, and water. By controlling temperature, air quality, and light, you achieve the moderate environment that is key to a successful greenhouse.

SITING AND ORIENTATION

Proper siting greatly affects greenhouse success. Essential considerations include:

■ Exposure to maximum sunlight. A greenhouse should receive at least six hours of sunlight every day, year-round. More is better. With less, you'll need supplemental lighting.

■ Orientation for maximum sun. On a sunny day, a greenhouse oriented with the long side east to west can capture 5 to 10 percent more light than one situated north to south.

■ Minimum exposure to wind. If you live in a windy area, consider planting a windbreak on the north side of your greenhouse. You may also want an especially sturdy greenhouse.

■ Adequate drainage with minimal slope. The best greenhouse location allows the floor to be raised slightly above ground level and pitched for water to drain out the door.

■ Stable soil. Building on boggy or sandy soil entails extra foundation work.

■ Convenient proximity to the house and storage areas, and to utilities for hookups.

■ Visual appeal, especially from the house, but also from neighbors' houses, the street, and viewpoints within your landscape.

FINDING THE SUNNIEST SPOT IN YOUR YARD

inding the sunniest spot on your property for your greenhouse will pay big dividends in success over many years. By using the following procedure, you can determine the areas of maximum year-round sunlight in your yard with a great deal of precision.

You will need access to the Internet. Assemble drawing paper, pencils and erasers, a T square, a protractor for drawing angles, and a ruler for measuring distance to scale and drawing straight lines. Make a base plan of your site with the size and location of sunblockers (such as trees and buildings) drawn to scale. The plan should show the exact direction of north. Then follow these steps:

1. Consult an atlas or the Internet to find the *latitude* and *longitude* of your location. An excellent site is www.census.gov/cgi-bin/gazetteer.

2. Consult the Internet at www.susdesign.com/sunangle/ and use your latitude and longitude to find out the *solar azimuth angles* (the angle of the sun from a line drawn north to south, which will give you the angle of the shadows on your plan) and the *solar altitude angles* (the height of the sun, which will help determine the length of shadows) for five times of the day on December 21: 8:30 a.m., 10 a.m., noon, 2 p.m., and 4 p.m.

3. Estimate and record the height of all sunblocking objects on your plan.

4. On a separate sheet of paper, draw a horizontal baseline. On this baseline, at the same scale as your ground plan, draw an elevation (side view) of each sunblocking object. Then, using your protractor, draw a line from the top left corner of each object to the baseline at the solar altitude angle you noted for 8:30 a.m. on December 21. The distance between the edge of an object and the point where its altitude-angle line crosses the baseline is the length of that object's shadow at 8:30 a.m.

5. On the plan, draw a line off to one side that runs exactly north and south; then use your protractor to draw another line intersecting the north-south line at the correct azimuth angle for 8:30 a.m. on December 21. Use this reference to draw parallel shading lines at exactly the same angle from each sunblocking object on the ground plan.

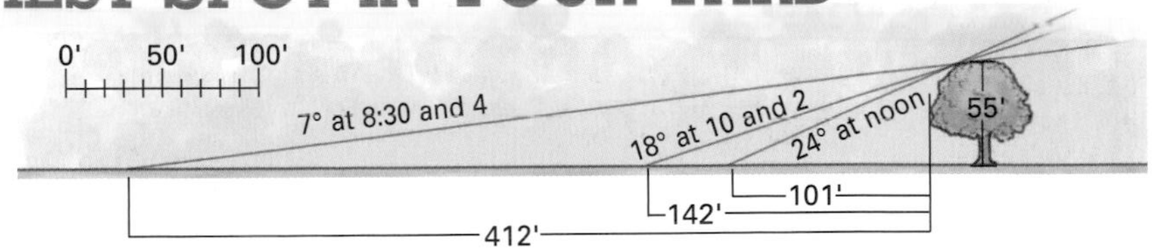

Above: Calculating the length of shadows of a 55-foot tree using solar altitude angles for five times of the day on December 21 (see step 4, at left). The home depicted is at latitude 41°32'N and longitude 93°39'W.

6. Mark off the length of the shadow of each object, as determined in step 4. Draw along the outer edge of each shadow, then erase all extra lines.

7. Repeat steps 4, 5, and 6 on the same ground plan for each object, and for all five times of the day on December 21, overlaying the shadows on top of one another. The result is a graphic prediction of where shadows will fall in your yard on the day of the year when they are the longest in the Northern Hemisphere. The most open areas on your diagram have the most year-round sunlight. The areas where shadows overlap one another the most will have the least amount of sun.

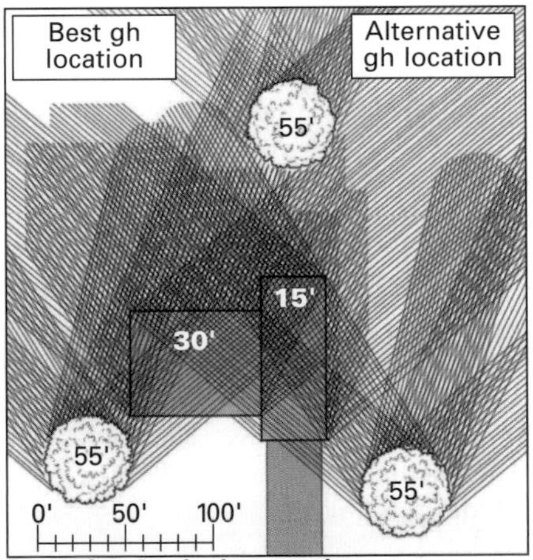

December 21 shadow overlay

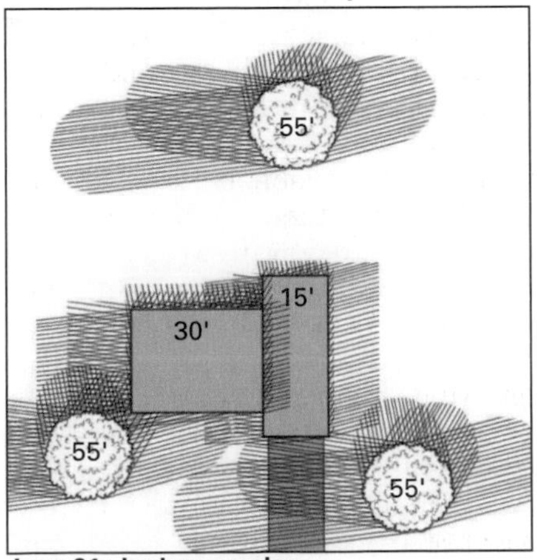

June 21 shadow overlay

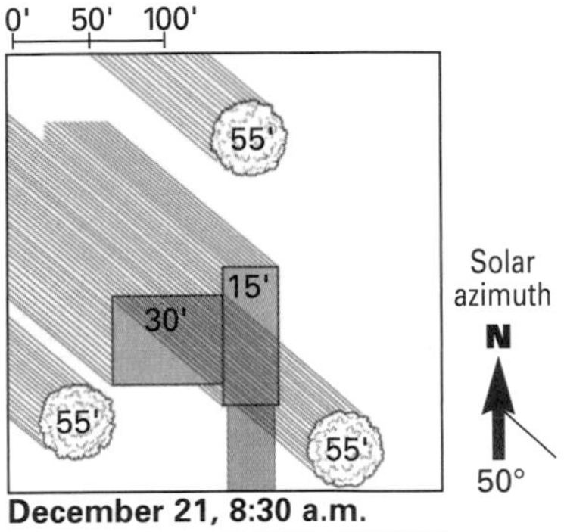

December 21, 8:30 a.m.

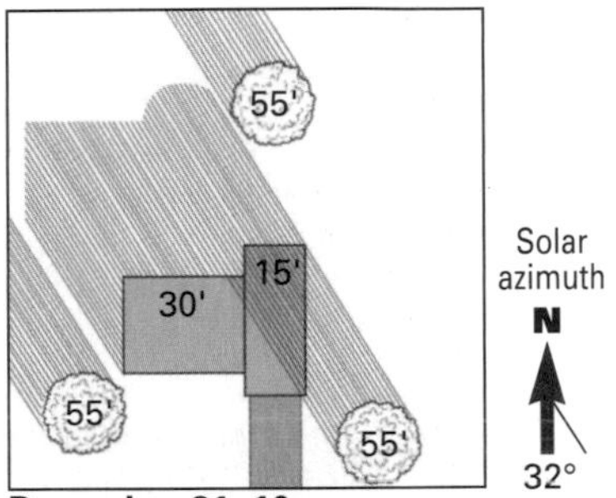

December 21, 10 a.m.

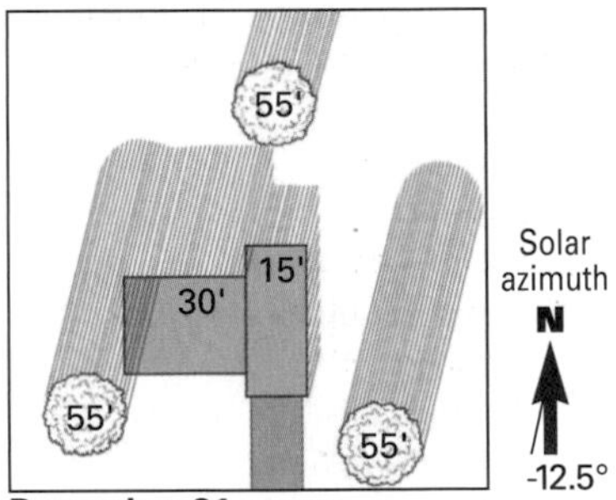

December 21, noon

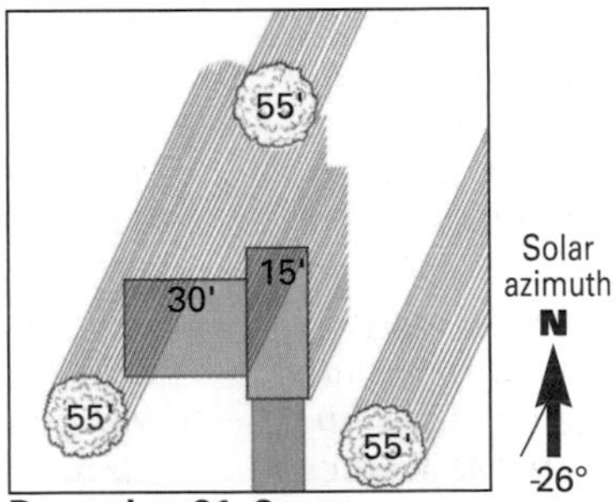

December 21, 2 p.m.

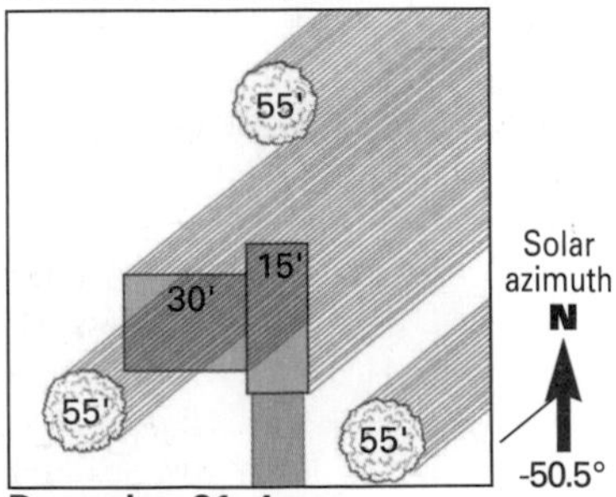

December 21, 4 p.m.

ATTACHED GREENHOUSES

Greenhouses can be categorized as either freestanding or attached—a distinction that simply notes their placement either as a separate structure or one connected to an existing building. Each type has qualities to recommend it, as well as potential drawbacks. Consider them all when selecting which kind of greenhouse to build.

ADVANTAGES AND USES OF ATTACHED DESIGNS

The brick sidewall on this attached greenhouse blends well with the adjoining house wall, producing a nice design touch with practical uses. The dark brick acts as a solar sink to store heat daily for release overnight. A greenhouse may also be attached to a garage, utility shed, or other building.

Greenhouses attached to the house offer the conveniences of home connected to the plant-growing space. You can pop in to check on a seed flat and go right back to stir the soup. Sources of water, warmth, and cooling are already nearby and are usually easily connected to the greenhouse. The accessibility of attached greenhouses as well as their potential for enhancing the house make them popular both in new construction and as home additions.

The challenges of building an attached greenhouse are the same as those of every addition: to design a new room that complements the house, and to be sure the structures and systems tie together without leaks. Because the greenhouse joins the house, its roof and ridge must easily shed rain, snow, and fallen leaves. The size and style of the attached greenhouse must relate directly to those of the home. For example, you may want a graceful Gothic curve to slope gently, but a low eave and the hot summer sun may call for a lower profile.

Some attached designs join the home only along an outside wall, using that wall for insulation and to tie in utilities. A-frames used this way can be adapted to a variety of wall heights, and doors at either end allow access and ventilation. Attached greenhouses that connect with a door or a window to the interior of the home—especially those in very mild climates—may need little additional heat because they open into heated rooms.

Another sort of attached greenhouse is gaining attention—solid-roof additions with clear greenhouse walls. These offer an attractive style by extending the home's roof, but they may require supplemental lighting to offset the loss of overhead sunlight.

SUNROOMS AND WINDOW GREENHOUSES

Sunrooms and conservatories present viable if somewhat limited spaces to grow houseplants. They make attractive and often satisfying additions, and may serve to whet your appetite to build a true greenhouse. This book intentionally does not offer plans for sunrooms or conservatories because they are designed primarily for the comfort of people, and their construction is handled differently.

The best location for a sunroom is a southern exposure, but it will likely need shade in summer. Plan for blinds, shutters, or curtains in your design, and include furniture that can recover from the occasional splash or spilled flowerpot. An eastern or northern exposure will work, but you will want to choose plants that tolerate low light conditions. Because a sunroom caters to the comfort of people, it is less humid and slightly cooler than a traditional greenhouse. The environment isn't ideal for some projects, such as starting seeds and rooting cuttings.

Fortunately, you can use plastic enclosures and additional light sources to enhance the conditions.

A window greenhouse is more than a collection of plants in a bay window, because it can be closed off from the house. The greenhouse effect tends to multiply in such a small, sunny space. Put a thermometer in the window greenhouse and watch it carefully; use the inside window as a vent when necessary. Use the window greenhouse to start seeds, root cuttings, pamper African violets, and grow herbs to snip all winter. A window greenhouse begs you to hang a prism to toss sunlight's rainbows all over the kitchen or breakfast room.

Sunrooms and window greenhouses can be included in new house construction, or built later as remodeling projects or home additions. As with greenhouses, you can build yours from a plan or a kit. Consult greenhouse manufacturers' catalogs for prefabricated models.

FREESTANDING GREENHOUSES

Freestanding greenhouses can be as large as the site allows, and they offer maximum exposure to the sun. Their height and shape depend on your design choices and can be adapted for sites and plants. On a practical level, freestanding greenhouses can be adapted to provide better drainage, adjust to difficult slopes, and accommodate shelving or ceiling rods for large plant collections. You can build up the foundation on one end, install drainage pipes in the floor, and even recycle irrigation water. You can vary the foundation height as necessary to put the greenhouse over a steep slope. Plants staged on shelves and hung from bars need a tall space with maximum sunlight; freestanding greenhouses are usually easier to design with generous headroom.

Any structure that stands alone requires its own systems for heating, cooling, and water supply, which may increase initial costs and operating expenses. Because your sunniest location will no doubt be its home, a freestanding greenhouse may take away from potential garden beds, and the distance from the house may become an issue in foul weather. On the other hand, for some gardeners, leaving a busy household to tend plants may be a welcome respite.

The need to heat and cool freestanding greenhouses independently sometimes leads gardeners to reject them, but consider the long-term advantages of separate systems. Any home addition, whether a greenhouse or a playroom, means increased utility costs and may also demand the addition of another system to perform adequately. It may be a trade-off: The cost of the additional utilities, heat, and vents needed in a freestanding

Building a freestanding greenhouse allows you to place It where the sun shines longest on the property, and to orient it with the longest side facing south to capture maximum sunlight.

greenhouse may be no higher than the cost of upgrading the existing system, if it is to work well enough to keep temperatures comfortable in the home and the greenhouse at the same time.

Some greenhouse chores, such as repotting large plants, will be much easier with more space. If it becomes necessary to use chemical sprays in the greenhouse, their odors may be less offensive in a separate space. Nongardening family members will especially appreciate less dirt and fewer strong smells drifting into living areas.

COLD FRAMES AND HOTBEDS

Cold frames and hotbeds put the greenhouse effect to work on a much smaller scale. They have similar uses—mostly starting seeds and extending the vegetable growing season—and similar construction. The difference between the two is that hotbeds have deeper sides to accommodate a source of bottom heat, usually manure or a buried heating cable. Collecting the sun's rays in a box of either sort can be very efficient, and venting the boxes during the day is crucial to using them successfully. See page 31 for instructions on building cold frames and hotbeds.

GREENHOUSE STYLES

Greenhouses have distinct styles set first by the roofline, then by the presence or absence of sidewalls and a foundation. Each style makes its statement in the landscape and plays a role in defining use.

The roofline of your greenhouse may come to a sharp peak, or incorporate a smooth arch from the ridge down to the ground or sidewall. Although either style can be covered with a variety of materials, a sturdily framed peaked roof on an A-frame or a barn-style greenhouse can best support glass panes. Any of the arched roofs are more suited to plastic film or other flexible coverings; some require less construction overall, so they can be less expensive to build. Peaked-roof and arched-roof styles can both be single-sloped, with a roof on only one side of the peak and a wall or attached building on the other.

Any style of greenhouse can be built with or without knee walls—solid walls that extend from the ground up to the height of benches. Knee walls lend a permanent appearance and enable you to add insulation at ground level that can reduce heating costs. However, a greenhouse without knee walls lets in more light and often requires less foundation work.

Peaked-roof greenhouses discussed in this book include A-frames (classic, modified, and sun-pit) and barn styles (straight- and slant-sided). Arched-roof greenhouses include the hoop and Gothic-arch greenhouses. Single-slope greenhouses are represented by the attached lean-to, attached angled-wall, and attached solar greenhouses, as well as cold frames and hotbeds.

A-FRAME GREENHOUSES deserve their reputation for simplicity. The walls and roof can be built in sections on the ground, then raised and joined together. The slope of the roof can vary but is steep enough to shed snow and rain. The classic A-frame is joined directly to the foundation. Headroom is at a premium in this style, and it can be hard to find room for hanging plants. Some A-frames solve this problem by resting on vertical sidewalls that provide a wider roof angle with extra venting, insulation, and headroom.

BARN-STYLE GREENHOUSES also come to a peak. In the barn style, an eave at the roof's edge connects the roof to a sidewall that can be slanted or vertical. That wall can drop down into a knee wall, but the barn style's inherent design strength doesn't demand one. The modified peak of the barn style spreads out to meet the eave, providing more headroom than a classic A-frame on the same size foundation. The ridge and upright walls also offer more obvious places for vents.

ARCHED-ROOF GREENHOUSES have design lines that contrast with traditional home construction and complement the garden's winding paths and garden beds. They can be built with or without knee walls. The simplest and least expensive structure is the hoop greenhouse. Its roofline looks like an upside-down U. In the Gothic arch, the curved side pieces form the roof's peak where they attach to a ridge board—a more elaborate construction that offers room for excellent ventilation systems. Attached aluminum-frame greenhouses with arched roofs generally let in more sunlight than wooden lean-to designs; both the narrower framing material and the curve of the roof work to the grower's advantage.

SINGLE-SLOPE GREENHOUSES can be thought of as greenhouses divided in half lengthwise along the ridgeline. Nearly all attached greenhouse styles present a single slope to the sun; some freestanding greenhouses also have this design or a modification in which the northern slope is reduced. When considering this style, remember that the northern slope admits as much as 10 percent of the sunlight entering a greenhouse—especially on overcast days when light is diffused. This may be relatively unimportant in the miniversions of single-slope greenhouses known as cold frames and hotbeds, but can be a significant loss of sunlight in larger single-slope greenhouses.

CLIMATIC CONCERNS IN DESIGNING YOUR GREENHOUSE

Seasonal weather extremes may lead you directly to a greenhouse style choice.

■ In cold-winter climates, a steeply sloped roof prevents ice and snow buildup, and a sturdy sidewall increases insulation opportunities.

■ Freestanding structures in windy sites demand additional bracing. In some cases, attached greenhouses may be more efficient to build and operate.

■ If heavy snowfall and howling winds prevail, a sun pit may be the most economical to operate. Because of its natural insulation, it requires less heat.

■ Where spring is short and the weather quickly warms up, a temporary greenhouse can be stored for reuse. A wide-span, low-profile roof will reduce heat buildup inside.

■ If torrential rains or heavy leaf fall can be expected, a steeply sloped A-frame design (which usually means no sidewalls) will allow the material to slide off fastest.

■ In rainy climates with reduced sunlight, attached greenhouses make access mud-free, and electricity for supplemental lighting is nearby.

■ Warm locations will benefit from designs that include floor-level vents common in barn-style greenhouses.

Low-cost hoop greenhouses are fast and easy to construct. See page 32.

Classic A-frames have steep sides that shed snow, rain, and leaves. See page 34.

The Gothic-arch greenhouse also sheds snow and is inexpensive. See page 36.

The wide roof and high walls of the modified A-frame offer good headroom. See page 38.

Sun pits begin with a backhoe and use earth for insulation. See page 40.

Barn-style greenhouses often use a solid sidewall for insulation. See page 42.

The slant-sided barn style offers a wide, sunny span. See page 44.

Attached lean-to greenhouses have a sloping roof that joins straight walls. See page 46.

The attached angled-wall style maximizes the low winter sun. See page 48.

Attached solar greenhouses can help heat your home. See page 50.

KIT GREENHOUSES OR CUSTOM PLANS

Elegant curved roof panels are often a feature of greenhouse kits. In many cases, the sunniest, most convenient location for an attached greenhouse is so sheltered from prevailing breezes that good air circulation is a problem. But greenhouse kits include options that improve ventilation, such as the louvered doors and windows on this one.

GREENHOUSE KIT COMPONENTS

All greenhouse kits begin with a frame, but there the similarities end. A close comparison is essential to a wise purchase. Compare the weight of the frame in similar size models; the heavier the gauge of the frame, the sturdier it is likely to be. Look for rustproof frames that include prehung doors, have a ventilation system, and are predrilled to simplify assembly. Kits with less prefabrication will be less expensive to purchase but more labor-intensive to construct.

Kits offer a variety of designs and coverings, sometimes as individual models in a catalog. Some catalogs have charts that show cover choices available on a particular style. Most hobby greenhouses today have rigid or flexible plastic coverings, often in multiple layers. Glass, long considered the finest greenhouse cover, may be less expensive than some insulated plastic materials but is more difficult to install. Choose the frame style that best suits your taste and landscape, but select a covering based on its expected longevity and maintenance in your climate.

Any kit you consider should include all hardware, detailed instructions, and a toll-free number for support, should you need it. Be sure to open your kit upon arrival, go over the packing list, and inventory the contents. Report any missing parts immediately.

KINDS OF KITS AND THEIR ADVANTAGES

Just about any style or type of greenhouse imaginable is available in kit form. Greenhouse supply catalogs offer choices in size, framing materials, and coverings that range widely in price and quality. Order several catalogs from the list on page 92 and carefully consider their offerings.

In many top-of-the-line kits, all structural components are predrilled, and the panels are cut to size or preassembled. Construction consists of following directions closely and assembling the parts. Mid-price kits call for more carpentry skills, such as making cuts and minor adjustments to the structure. You can also purchase sets of plans or just the greenhouse frame to assemble yourself, and use locally available coverings. Remember that whether you buy a kit or build a greenhouse from scratch, you will still need to provide a foundation and utility hookups.

When two kits have similar components, the freestanding one will be easier to build; attaching a prefabricated greenhouse to an existing house can be complicated. Unless the kit greenhouse fits perfectly and you have the skills to seal and weatherproof it, you may develop problems only a professional can solve. The freestanding kit greenhouse can be more forgiving to build, and its location away from the house makes it less of a focal point. Many freestanding kits also offer modular expansions; when you're ready for more room, you take off one wall and add another section.

Properly built kit greenhouses look finished, even elegant, right away. Their metal ribs, sleek lines, and construction details have the advantage of field testing by the manufacturer.

Kit greenhouses are basic structures; you must provide the equipment that maintains the environment. Consider your kit supplier as a source for accessories such as heaters and fans; adding your own may require changes in the structure that could affect warranties. Read all the literature from kit suppliers closely, and consult them directly for more information and to find out what customer support is available.

Installing utilities for a greenhouse requires careful planning and often the assistance of professionals. Kit plans suggest placements that are the most efficient for that space. Other necessities, such as benches, fertilizer, and irrigation systems, are also available from kit suppliers.

BUILDING A GREENHOUSE YOURSELF, OR HIRING LABOR

When planning a greenhouse, study several plans or kit models closely to find one where the labor needed fits your capabilities. The added expense of a precut and predrilled kit may be offset by the cost of hiring someone to do those steps for you. You may decide to hire someone to help dig the foundation, hold up walls, and hoist fans into place. Or you may elect to do everything except the wiring yourself. Whatever work plan you evolve, make sure it suits your ability.

Your plan should include a division of tasks you will do and those you will hire out. Get estimates for each phase and for the total project to compare as you make a work plan.

ASSESSING BUILDING SKILLS

Labor is divided into four basic categories—manual, basic carpentry, skilled carpentry, and utility work (including wiring, plumbing, and hookups). Building a greenhouse involves all four. Whether you do them yourself or work with a contractor, it is essential that you evaluate each. Tasks such as digging the foundation, hauling lumber and dirt, laying pipe, pouring concrete, raising framed sides, and lifting equipment require a strong back.

Most kits demand only the most basic carpentry skills, such as reading directions, squaring up, and using a level, hammer, and screwdriver. The simplest custom plans require these skills plus the ability to drill some holes and make simple cuts in lumber or pipe. As the complexity of greenhouse plans increases, their demand for skilled carpentry grows to include cutting angles, hanging doors and vents, and installing automatic systems.

WORKING WITH A CONTRACTOR

Even if your skills are strong in all these areas, customizing a plan or attaching a greenhouse may require that you consult a professional. One design change seldom stands alone: An extended wall means more stress on the roof; tacking on a potting shed may demand more heat for the whole structure. Attaching a greenhouse may be the biggest design change you ever make to your home; your priority should be a seal that is totally weatherproof and aesthetically attractive. Utility installation and wiring often require the services of professionals in order to comply with local regulations and safety codes—as well as meet the requirements of your insurer. Hiring an experienced contractor can often save you time, aggravation—and even money.

Standard greenhouse plans can be adapted when you design and build your own structure. If bricklaying isn't one of your talents, change the sidewalls to concrete blocks or a wooden frame.

CUTTING COSTS

Sometimes the greenhouse of your dreams simply costs too much, but there may be alternatives. Buying a used greenhouse and reassembling it on your property lets you see the house first as well as save money. Recycled materials can be another way to cut costs; use the sink and door left over from remodeling your kitchen, for instance.

To comply with building codes and zoning restrictions, you may want to consult an architect or a builder, and then do the work yourself in stages. Perhaps you can install a foundation now, but put a simple A-frame greenhouse on it while you save for that elegant arched-roof style you really want. Developing creative strategies can help you meet your needs—and dreams.

COST FACTORS TO COMPARE

Price will seldom be the final consideration in choosing to buy a kit or assemble the parts for the greenhouse yourself, but there are other variables to consider. A good kit contains the precut and predrilled frame, its covering and door, and all the hardware to assemble it and attach the covering. The kit price does not include shipping costs, so figure the freight before you compare the kit cost to materials purchased locally. In pricing lumber or other framing materials, you must estimate the inevitable waste and overage as a real cost. You will also buy slightly more covering material and hardware for the same reasons. The veteran do-it-yourselfer's rule calls for no more than 5 percent excess; less experienced folks should allow for 10 percent.

Kits usually do not include equipment or accessories, but read the kit warranty closely. You may save money by acquiring such items as heaters, fans, and vents from other sources, but those installations may invalidate some structural warranties.

CONSTRUCTION BASICS

Whether you build your greenhouse from scratch or a kit, or whether you do the work yourself, supervise someone else, or hire a contractor, an understanding of construction basics will help make your project more successful. This chapter includes information about building a greenhouse foundation and frame; choosing and installing covers, floors, vents, and equipment for heating and ventilation; hooking up utilities; and using solar energy.

GREENHOUSE FOUNDATIONS

The type of foundation your greenhouse needs will depend on several factors, including the model you choose to build, the materials you use, and your local climate. If you live in an area where the ground freezes during the winter and you intend to cover your greenhouse with panes of glass, its foundation will need to reach below the frost line to prevent damage caused when the ground freezes and heaves. In far northern areas, that will be several feet below ground, requiring a concrete footing and concrete-block or poured concrete foundation. In milder climates, where the frost reaches only a few inches below the surface, a foundation of poured concrete or concrete blocks 6 to 8 inches deep or a foundation anchored to posts or piers is enough to support the structure. In a mild climate, a lightly framed, plastic-covered greenhouse can sit on a ground-level foundation of treated lumber. In any case, the foundation must secure the greenhouse firmly to the ground to withstand strong winds. The foundation must be level and square if the greenhouse walls and roof are to fit properly.

SITE PREPARATION

The first task in construction is to mark the location of the foundation. On the site you have selected for your greenhouse, measure the dimensions precisely and mark the corners with 2-foot-tall wooden 2×2 stakes. Make certain the perimeter is square by

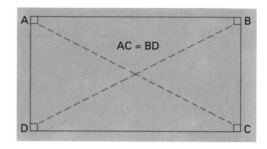

measuring the diagonals, as shown in the diagram above. The diagonals should be equal; if not, adjust your layout and remeasure. String lines from stake to stake.

If you are going to build a concrete foundation, put up batter boards at the four corners of the marked perimeter, as follows: At each corner, drive three 2×4 stakes 2 feet outside the corner stake—one directly on the diagonal from the opposite corner, with the other two stakes 4 feet from the first stake down each side of the perimeter. Check the newly formed 90-degree angles with a large framing square. Now connect the stakes with 1×4 boards nailed level near the stake tops.

Next pull another set of strings directly above the original four strings. Make small cuts, called kerfs, in each of the batter boards to correspond with those original lines. Use a line level or water level to mark an equal elevation and attach the strings at each batter board. Finally, remove the original stakes and strings. You have created a square and level

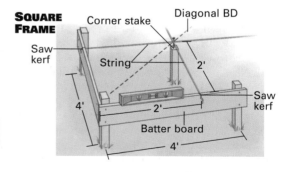

SQUARE FRAME

frame identical to the greenhouse site. The intersections of the strings mark the corners of the greenhouse.

If the site is fairly level to begin with, a shovel and wheelbarrow may be all you need to excavate for a level foundation. If one corner sits more than a few inches above another, or if you are working in an area where heavy soils or rocks make digging by hand impractical, consider renting a backhoe or hiring a grading professional to lower or raise the site to level.

CONCRETE FOUNDATIONS

Greenhouses that are subject to a hard winter freeze or are built on moist or loose soil need a poured concrete or concrete-block foundation. (They may also rest on piers or posts that extend below the frost line; see the box below.) Construction of a concrete foundation calls for digging a trench, pouring a footing, and building up the walls of a foundation.

If you plan to build a foundation knee wall, the footing under it needs to be 16 inches wide. For designs in which roof rafters are placed directly on the foundation, such as an A-frame, a 12-inch-wide footing is ample.

The first step in constructing a poured

concrete footing is to mark the batter boards on each side of their initial saw kerfs: 8 inches on each side of the kerfs for a 16-inch-wide footing, 6 inches on each side for a 12-inch-wide footing. Make additional cuts at these marks and pull strings all around. Use a plumb bob and drive smaller stakes at the

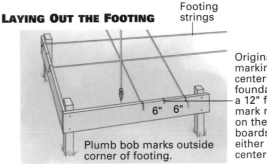

LAYING OUT THE FOOTING

Footing strings

Original kerf marking centerline of foundation. For a 12" footing, mark new kerfs on the batter boards 6" to either side of centerline kerf.

Plumb bob marks outside corner of footing.

inside and outside of each corner. Finally, outline the footing's path by snapping chalk lines or spraying lines on the ground, then remove all the strings.

The next step is to dig a trench in which the footing will sit. It should reach below the

WOODEN FRAME FOUNDATION

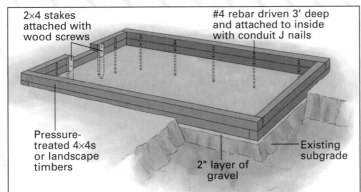

2×4 stakes attached with wood screws

#4 rebar driven 3' deep and attached to inside with conduit J nails

Pressure-treated 4×4s or landscape timbers

2" layer of gravel

Existing subgrade

A simple foundation can be constructed of treated lumber or landscaping timbers. This is a good option if a greenhouse is only temporary or may be moved.

Start with a level site; measure, square up, and mark the perimeter. Dig a trench 4 to 6 inches below grade on the perimeter, a couple of inches wider than your lumber. Fill with 2 inches of gravel. Stack the 4×4s or timbers on top of one another and fasten them with large galvanized deck screws. Check again for square and level.

To anchor to the ground, choose one of several options: Pound ½-inch reinforcing bar (#4 rebar) stakes 3 feet into the ground at the corners and every 4 feet along the inside of the foundation; attach the rebars with conduit J nails. Or drill holes through the timbers and drive L-shaped rebars through them into the ground. Or cut 2×4 stakes and attach them with wood screws. Another option is to use screw-type fence anchors (see page 34).

WOODEN POST FOUNDATION

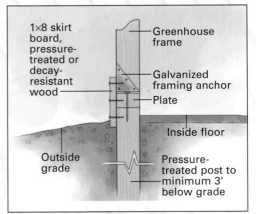

1×8 skirt board, pressure-treated or decay-resistant wood

Greenhouse frame

Galvanized framing anchor

Plate

Inside floor

Outside grade

Pressure-treated post to minimum 3' below grade

Pressure-treated posts provide a low-cost, simple base for wooden frame greenhouses. Use a posthole digger to dig the holes, or you may want to rent a power auger if you have many holes to dig. Holes should reach below the frost line. Contact local utilities to mark the location of cables or pipes before you dig.

Place 2 to 3 inches of gravel in the bottom of each hole. Leave a few extra inches on the height of the post; cut to length after it is set. Set the post; backfill with dirt, making sure the post is vertical and square with the foundation lines.

(For a more permanent set, use concrete.)

GREENHOUSE FOUNDATIONS
continued

frost line. If you will be building directly on top of the foundation, the wooden sill should be at least 4 inches above the finished grade.

Where the frost line is shallow, you may need only a poured footing; you can build directly on it. When a heavier foundation is needed, you should build a concrete footing and wall. That requires two steps: Pour the footing, and then build up the wall using concrete blocks.

If the soil is not sandy or loose, the sides of the trench will serve as the form for the footing. Otherwise, you'll need forms to hold the concrete as it is poured. The footing itself should be about 6 inches deep. Lay two pieces of reinforcing bar (rebar) horizontally in the trench, supported 2 to 3 inches from the bottom by small bricks or stones. Forms are usually constructed from ½-inch plywood, braced by 2×4 lumber. Bracing the forms is important; concrete weighs more than 100 pounds per cubic foot. If you are building directly on the footing, add forms to extend the footing above ground; level them, and then pour the concrete.

TRENCH AND FORMS

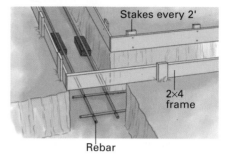

For all but the smallest projects, it is easier to have the concrete delivered. As it is being poured, work the mix frequently with a rod or stick to remove air bubbles. If you are going to attach the frame directly to the footing, insert anchor bolts (called J bolts). Placement and size of the bolts will vary with design and building materials; in general, place them within a foot of each corner and then every 4 feet. Make them perpendicular to the foundation, leaving 2½ inches of the threaded end exposed. Leave the forms in place for 48 to 72 hours.

If you choose to build a knee wall from concrete blocks, begin by following the steps

CONCRETE SLAB FOUNDATION

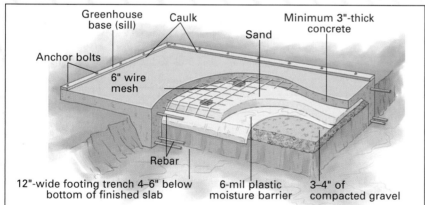

A slab foundation for a freestanding greenhouse provides flooring and structural support in one piece.

Prepare a square, level site. When finished, a freestanding floor should be 3 to 4 inches above grade. An attached slab should be even with or one or two steps below the house floor, and above grade. For most greenhouses, a 3-inch-thick floor is adequate. It will be poured on top of 3 to 4 inches of compacted gravel.

In addition, some local building codes may require a layer of sand. Clear the soil from your site to the appropriate depth. Dig a 12-inch-wide footing trench another 4 to 6 inches deep around the perimeter. Build 2×4 forms (see text above) around the perimeter so that the top is at the desired level. An attached slab should be sloped slightly away from the house for drainage. Lay rebar in the footing trench, held at

least 2 inches from the bottom by small stone blocks called dobies. Cover the slab area (not including the trench) with 3 to 4 inches of gravel. Place a 6-mil plastic moisture barrier on top of the rock. (If needed, add a layer of sand on top of the plastic.) Use dobies to support 6-inch wire mesh about 2 inches above the rock or sand.

Pour concrete first into the footing trenches; let it stiffen slightly, then pour across the floor area. Smooth with a concrete float and trowels, creating a slight slope or crown to provide water drainage. Insert anchor bolts (J bolts) for the sill while the concrete is still wet. Make sure they are vertical, and placed within 1 foot of each corner and about 4 feet apart along the sides. Keep the concrete moist for a few days until it is set. Then remove the forms, add sheets of 1- to 2-inch-thick rigid polystyrene insulation around the outside of the slab 1 to 2 feet deep, and backfill the trench.

ANCHORING THE SILL

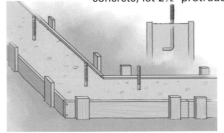

Set anchor bolt in wet concrete; let 2½" protrude.

to pour the footing, described on pages 15 and 16. Next, using a 2×2 board, trowel a keyway—a shallow channel 2 to 4 inches wide—down the middle of the footing. This will strengthen the connection of the wall to the footing.

to provide a nailing surface for the walls. Once the concrete has set, lay the sill board centered over the foundation, tap it to mark the bolts, and drill holes. Attach the sill to the anchor bolts with washers and nuts.

To create a smooth sill, countersink the washers and nuts into the board. You may need to cut the ends off the bolts.

ADDING THE SILL

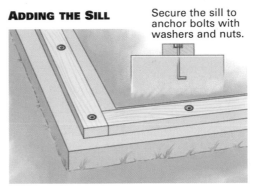

Secure the sill to anchor bolts with washers and nuts.

Step 2: Fill in courses of blocks.

The final step in building a foundation is adding the sill, a treated-wood board bolted horizontally on top of the footing or sidewall

CONCRETE BLOCK-AND-PIER FOUNDATIONS

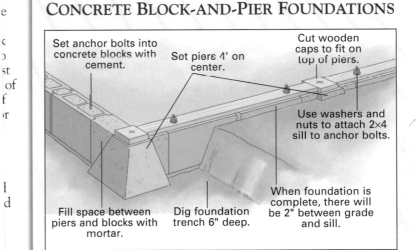

Set anchor bolts into concrete blocks with cement.

Set piers 4' on center.

Cut wooden caps to fit on top of piers.

Use washers and nuts to attach 2×4 sill to anchor bolts.

Fill space between piers and blocks with mortar.

Dig foundation trench 6" deep.

When foundation is complete, there will be 2" between grade and sill.

A simple foundation for greenhouses in mild climates can be built from a combination of concrete blocks and precast piers placed directly on firm ground. (Be sure to check your local building codes to see if this is acceptable.) Begin by digging a foundation trench about a foot wide and 4 to 6 inches deep around the perimeter line of your structure. As always, make sure your perimeter is square and the bottom of the trench is level. Set precast concrete piers in the corners, aligned and squared with the perimeter lines. Between piers, set standard concrete blocks in line, joining them with mortar mix.

Precast piers come ready-made to accept wooden posts or sills. Some have anchor bolts already set, some have metal brackets, some have rectangular grooves to accept dimensional lumber, and some have wooden caps already in place. Set anchor bolts along the rest of the wall, about 4 feet apart, by filling the hole of a block with concrete and inserting a J bolt. Once the concrete has set, mark a 2×4 or 2×6 sill board and drill holes to attach the sill to the bolts. You may add sheets of rigid insulation along the foundation before backfilling the trench.

PLUMBING AND WIRING

Planning for your greenhouse should include the location of the utilities—water, electricity, and fuel supply (such as gas). This factor may determine where you can locate the greenhouse, and whether it is attached or freestanding.

For a greenhouse attached to a home, the utilities are normally run from their source, along the ceiling and through the header above the foundation wall. For a detached greenhouse, the utilities may come from the same sources but should be buried outside, below ground in a trench, for both convenience and safety. (This gets them out of the way of the lawn mower, for one thing.) If you don't install plumbing hookups before you pour a concrete foundation, you may have to drill a hole in the foundation wall to accommodate a water pipe at a level below the frost line.

Water, gas, and electrical hookups are not projects for the novice do-it-yourselfer. Unless you are experienced, hire professionals to handle these jobs. However, you can take several steps that will save some money and ensure that contractors provide the services you need.

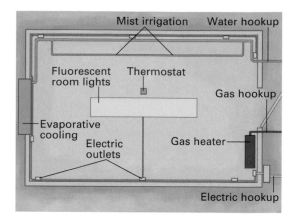

A typical layout for electric, gas, and water lines in a small greenhouse.

A more permanent installation for year-round use requires a supply pipe buried below the frost line. This requires digging a trench, laying the pipe, covering it with a couple of inches of sand, and backfilling and replacing the sod. Digging a trench is back-breaking work, especially if the frost line in your area is deeper than 2 feet. It may be better to hire out this part of the job. At the same time the workers could dig the trenches for the footing of the greenhouse if you are putting in a permanent foundation.

When you are putting in the water pipe, you can also install the electric wiring and gas line in the same trench. Check with the local utility company or the building inspector to determine the separating distances. Before you pour any concrete footings, place a piece of 4-inch or 6-inch pipe through the footing to accommodate the utilities later on.

WATER SUPPLY

Some growers can get by with a hose from the nearest faucet. Either roll up the hose between uses or bury it in a shallow trench just below the lawn surface to get it out of the way of the mower.

PIPE TYPES TO USE IN THE GREENHOUSE

Check local building codes for installation restrictions in your area. Whether you do it yourself or hire a professional, here are the kinds of materials most often used in greenhouse construction.

Utility	Material	Qualities	Buy As
Electrical conduit	Aluminum	Weatherproofing for cable	6' or 12' lengths
	Rigid plastic	Weatherproofing for cable	12' lengths
Plastic water pipe	CPVC	Cold and hot water supply	12' lengths
	PB	Cold and hot water supply, flexible, freezes often	12' lengths
	PVC	Rigid pipe, cold water only, use inside greenhouse only	12' lengths
Natural gas pipe	IP galvanized	Rigid, must thread and seal all joints	Cut to length
	Flexible gas	Connect heater inside	Buy shortest length

Rigid galvanized gas pipe

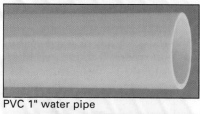

PVC 1" water pipe

Aluminum electrical conduit

The water needs of a hobby greenhouse are relatively modest. The size of the water pipe should be a minimum of ¾ inch, which will supply 5 to 6 gallons per minute (gpm), enough to supply one hose. For a larger greenhouse (over 500 square feet), or for a pipe length greater than 100 feet, it is better to install a 1-inch pipe, which will supply 10 to 12 gpm. This is adequate for most automated sprinkler systems.

The piping should be attached to a dry hydrant inside the greenhouse so that it can be drained if freezing temperatures occur. A dry hydrant is a hose faucet that drains the aboveground piping to a dry well below ground when shut off.

To prevent contamination of the home drinking water, a vacuum breaker should be installed on the hose faucet. This is required by most municipal water systems.

One hose faucet is usually adequate for hobby greenhouses. A second faucet or supply line may be necessary for a greenhouse over 500 square feet, if an evaporative cooling system will be installed, or if you will be installing a sink.

If you plan to install a sink, you will need to determine how to dispose of waste water. Connection to a septic system or sewer may be possible but may require a lot of trenching. An alternative may be a dry well, either manufactured or stone-filled. In any case, the sink should have a settling basin and trap to collect soil and other debris.

ELECTRIC SUPPLY

An electric supply in the greenhouse is needed to operate fans, heaters, lighting, and other equipment. The power source is usually the distribution panel in the home. Have an electrician check to see that there are enough extra circuits and capacity to supply the greenhouse.

For most small greenhouses of less than 500 square feet, a single 20-amp, 120-volt line provides adequate power for the fan, louver or vent motors, a room light, and the controls for a gas heater. For larger greenhouses, determine the wattage of each piece of electrical equipment and add these together to get the total need. If electric heat will be used, 240-volt service should be installed.

The cable between the electric box in the home and the greenhouse should be buried in the same trench as the water line. It should be waterproof and of adequate size to prevent excessive voltage drop.

Within the greenhouse the cable is attached to a distribution box that serves the different appliances. It should have a main switch and individual switches for each circuit. It is best to install the wiring to the different appliances in plastic conduit. Use waterproof outlet and switch boxes, because humidity levels are high. Outlets should be protected by a ground fault circuit interrupter (GFCI). One GFCI can protect a whole circuit if it is installed in the first box. A backup power supply is convenient if you are in an area where power outages occur frequently. It can save your valuable plants on a cold night. A 5,000-watt generator is adequate for most greenhouses and can also be used to power some of the appliances in the home. A double pole–double throw disconnect switch is needed if it will be attached to the power panel in the home. Install an alarm system that can indicate trouble in the greenhouse.

GAS SERVICE

If you are planning to heat your greenhouse with natural gas or propane, the supply piping should be installed by a licensed heating contractor. Natural gas is piped from the street or the meter near the house. Propane requires a storage tank near the greenhouse. The line should be brought into the greenhouse near where the heater will be located.

CODE ISSUES AND HIRING PROFESSIONALS

Safety must be your first concern when installing utilities. Building, plumbing, and wiring codes have been established in every municipality and must be followed. Most are based on the square footage to be built, but all contain minimum requirements for materials and procedures. Although some may seem arcane, and some will entail extra cost, codes were developed to promote public safety. Consult local authorities, obtain permits, and be sure the professionals you hire are licensed and bonded and work up to code. Even in areas where no building permit is required, the safe operation of your greenhouse over the years depends on careful plumbing and wiring done during construction.

Proper electrical grounding is essential in the moist environment of the greenhouse. To avoid dangerous shocks, each circuit should be ground-fault protected with a correctly installed GFCI outlet (shown above). Only one GFCI outlet per circuit is needed as long as it is the first outlet in the circuit.

FRAMING AND FLOORING

Frames can be constructed of wood, extruded metal, pipe (either metal or PVC), or even masonry. If you purchase a kit greenhouse, framing is a matter of following directions to bolt the walls and roof to the sill in the proper order. Most kits are precut, so the spaces for vents and doors are included. Building your own wooden frame will take time and patience, but it gives you the flexibility to customize the design.

Frame sections are assembled separately, then attached to a sill, house wall, or ledger board. A ledger board is used in an attached greenhouse; it is a 2×6 piece attached with lag screws to the studs along an existing wall. It functions just as a sill does, providing a nailing surface, usually for roof rafters (see page 46). Pieces of 2×4, called plates, are horizontal supports for attaching sidewall studs at the top and bottom. The lower plate attaches to the sill. Rafters lie across the plate at the top of the wall to form the roof. Plates and ledgers run the length of the house; rafters usually run its width. In a freestanding greenhouse, the rafters also attach to a ridge board to form the roof's peak.

Build each section of the frame with the pieces laid on a level surface, such as a garage floor or sheets of plywood; it's easier and helps keep the frame square as you nail it together.

Enlist a few people to help raise the frames, for safety's sake and to avoid dropping them and damaging the walls.

This frame is square and ready to cover. The floor will be gravel with a brick path.

FRAMING TIPS

Lumber comes in standard lengths: 8, 10, 12, 14, and 16 feet. When estimating what you need, include some extra and use the overage for braces and attaching coverings.

Learn to use a framing square. One side of it is the same width as a 2×4, providing a handy measure of width, as well as square.

Keep the greenhouse frame steady as you build. Stand on one stud while nailing on the plate to keep the frame from shifting under your feet.

Treated lumber works best for greenhouse construction. It resists insect and water damage. Increase its durability, as well as light reflection in the greenhouse, by painting all wood with a good quality white latex paint.

FRAMING WALLS

The dimensions of your greenhouse will determine the lengths to cut for plates, rafters, and studs for the front and end walls, but all of the measurements will be based on the actual sizes of dimensional lumber.

For example, for a 6-foot vertical wall, cut the studs 5 feet 9 inches long to allow 3 inches for the top and bottom plates (a 2× piece of lumber is actually 1½ inches thick). Plan to put a stud every 2 feet on center. Because a 2×4 stud is actually 3½ inches wide, you will need to cut the plates for the end walls accordingly; that is, subtract 3½ inches for each piece. For example, the plates on the 8-foot end wall of a freestanding greenhouse will be 7 feet 5 inches long. (Other plans may use a different stud spacing and may not utilize a top plate.)

To lay out the wall, put the top and bottom plates side by side flat on a level surface. Use a framing square so you can make marks 2 feet apart on both plates at the same time; that enables you to line up the studs properly, which will help ensure a sturdy frame.

Lay out all the walls of a structure in the same way. Nail together the plates and studs of each wall. When you raise the walls, use a level frequently to keep the studs vertical while you nail and brace each wall to the foundation and to the other walls.

FRAMING DOORS AND VENTS

Most greenhouses have doors and louvers in the end wall, with vents added in the sides and often along the roof ridge. To allow for doors and vents, leave an opening in the frame as wide as these components plus ¼ inch. If these openings do not leave enough space for studs on 2-foot centers, move the studs closer together or farther apart, but do not eliminate a stud in the frame for the sake of a door or vent. Bridge the opening with a horizontal brace called a header.

You can build a door to fit, or make the frame fit a ready-made storm door. A custom door is just that; you can build it to compensate for limited end wall height in an attached greenhouse or wide enough to allow a wheelchair and garden cart easy access. Storm doors can be purchased ready to install; those with screened windows in them offer welcome additional ventilation. In either case, you will top the door opening with a 2×4 header that runs the width of the wall.

Doors will be more stable if additional braces are added between the door frame and the adjacent studs.

Vents, too, can be built on site or purchased in convenient sizes and installed. They can be as simple as frames covered in the same plastic as the rest of the house, or purchased ready-made, equipped with shutters, shades, or louvers. As their weight increases, so will the need for additional bracing around their frames.

FRAMING THE ROOF

A roof frame usually uses 2×4 rafters on 2-foot centers that line up with studs in the wall. Larger lumber, such as 2×6s, may be needed for longer spans or in a heavy snow locale. Rafters are nailed to the top of the plates and to the ridge board at the roof's peak, or to a ledger board with metal joist hangers. Start the roof by laying out one rafter and marking it to achieve a workable slope and proper fit. Individual greenhouse plans provide ways to measure an appropriate angle. Cut one rafter, check it against your plans and dimensions, and use it as a pattern to cut the others.

At the ends of the roof, double up the rafters to provide additional nailing surfaces to attach a covering. To stabilize and strengthen a roof, cut short lengths of 2×4 to nail in as braces between the rafters.

FLOORING MATERIALS

The easiest way to floor a greenhouse is simply to leave bare ground, prepare the soil, and use part of it for planting. To avoid mud, bring in flagstone, pavers, or raised slats for a path. Weeds can become a problem; use weed barrier cloth to shade out unwelcome sprouts. (Do not use plastic; it will impede drainage.)

Gravel is an inexpensive flooring choice. A layer 3 to 4 inches deep is easy to install and keeps mud and weeds at bay. You can water freely in the greenhouse and let the water run into the gravel, where it will help increase humidity.

If you choose a loose material, such as gravel, bark, bricks, pavers, or a combination of these, prepare the floor space first. Clear the area completely and cover it with weed barrier cloth before installing the floor. Use sand as a base for bricks or pavers, or simply shovel gravel or bark onto the barrier cloth.

Some greenhouse owners build a concrete walk or a full slab under the structure. It takes more work to install but offers distinct advantages. Its surface is smooth and easy to clean, it reflects light, and it holds some heat. If you need a clean environment for starting seeds, a concrete floor can help cut

WOOD FOR GREENHOUSES

The wood you use to build your greenhouse must last for years. Use either foundation-grade redwood or pressure-treated lumber that has been impregnated with wood preservative chemicals. Foundation-grade redwood in contact with the soil can last up to 15 years. Pressure-treated wood can last a lifetime. Look for wood treated with naturally occurring chemicals that produce no fumes or leachates. Do not use oil-based products such as creosote; they release fumes harmful to plants.

down on diseases that can breed in open-soil areas.

The choices you make in flooring materials affect your flexibility in using greenhouse space. Permanent materials, such as mortared pavers or concrete, offer a stable floor on which benches, storage cabinets, sinks, and hoses can stay put where you will use them for years. Once a permanent floor is installed, you're done with it; maintenance is a simple matter of seasonal cleaning.

Changeable flooring materials, such as gravel or bark, provide more options over time. Their advantage is adaptability to your growing habits. You can change the floor with a shovel, removing rock and adding soil for a bed. Maintenance includes raking to smooth the covering and replacing the materials from time to time.

SLOPE AND DRAINAGE

Plan the slope of the greenhouse floor so water will drain out and away from the structure, if it has hard-surface flooring such as a concrete pad. A drop of 1/8 to 1/4 inch per linear foot is adequate. Standing water creates hazardous conditions for plants and people. It harbors pathogens, lends a chill in winter, breeds mosquitoes in summer, and can cause dangerous slips and falls.

It is especially important that a solid concrete floor be contoured when it is poured to create a slight slope or a crown to shed water. In addition, concrete, tile, or brick should have a rough finish that is not slippery when wet.

Clear weeds from floor areas, then install weed barrier cloth (never plastic) underneath gravel and pavers.

GREENHOUSE COVERINGS

Tempered glass is long-lasting, provides excellent transmission of light, and looks stylish.

Tempered glass

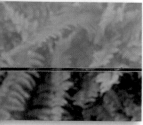

Double-strength glass

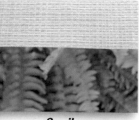

8-mil woven poly ("rip-stop")

One of the most important decisions you will make is the choice of material for the greenhouse cover. The ideal covering lets in the maximum amount of light while allowing the least amount of heat to escape. It should also be durable and require a minimum of maintenance.

Visible light transmission for common glazing materials varies from 78 percent to 93 percent. One rule: During winter, for every 1 percent reduction in light that a plant receives, there will be a 1 percent reduction in plant growth. Your selection of a covering material should be made with care.

Sunlight passing through glazing can be either direct, which causes shadows, or diffuse, which creates a more uniform light pattern. In areas that have significant cloudy weather, the light is already diffuse and the type of glazing is not as critical.

GLASS

Glass is a traditional covering material for greenhouses, and it rates high for direct light transmission and durability. Glass with coatings and tints, however, should be used with caution. As can be seen from the table on page 23, low-E (low emission), heat-mirror, and bronze-tinted glass can significantly reduce light transmission.

The glass used on today's hobby greenhouses is tempered to increase its strength. This allows use of panes 30 to 36 inches wide, which reduces the number of glazing bars required and increases light transmission. Such larger panes of glass are usually installed using rubber gaskets rather than caulking.

POLYCARBONATE

This material is available as a single-layer corrugated glazing or as a double- or triple-wall structured sheet. All are flexible and will bend over curved surfaces of large radius. The material is clear, providing high light transmission. Polycarbonates have high impact resistance to protect from hail and vandalism, and are less flammable than other plastic materials. They can be purchased already coated with a wetting agent that reduces dripping of moisture. Sheets are normally 4 feet wide; many lengths are available.

Polycarbonate materials expand and contract with temperature change. Installation must allow for this. Single-layer material is usually installed with screws and a rubber gasket. Wood or foam seals are used around the edges. Double- and triple-layer material is attached to the greenhouse frame with plastic or aluminum "h" or "H" extrusions. The top and bottom of the sheet should be sealed with aluminum tape to keep out dust, insects, and algae. A bead of silicone caulk along the edge of the extrusion will keep out water.

ACRYLIC

Acrylic is a little more clear than polycarbonate but yellows slowly with age. It is flammable and not generally approved for institutional greenhouses. Acrylic glazing attracts dust and dirt more readily than polycarbonate, and it scratches more easily.

Acrylic structured sheets are available in several thicknesses. The material is rigid and must be installed on flat surfaces. Installation techniques are similar to those for polycarbonate sheets using the aluminum extrusions to allow for expansion.

FIBERGLASS-REINFORCED PLASTIC (FRP)

Fiberglass, although still available, has generally been replaced by other materials, mainly polycarbonate. This is because the plastic resin that coats the glass fibers erodes after a few years, and the glazing becomes dark from the dust and dirt that are picked up. Recoating involves washing the fiberglass and painting on a single layer of plastic resin.

Flat sheeting fiberglass is a good choice for end wall glazing. Purchase the clear material. It comes in rolls, 3 or 4 feet wide by 25 or 50 feet long. It should be attached with rubber-gasketed screws to allow for expansion. When installing corrugated fiberglass panels as roofing, use corrugated molding at the top and bottom and half-moon spacers on cross braces to minimize dripping from condensation.

PLASTIC FILM

Light weight, large sheet size, and low cost make plastic film a good choice for hobby greenhouses used for seasonal production of crops. It is a good choice for hoop houses because it can conform to the curved shape. Greenhouse-grade plastics with ultraviolet (UV) protection have been developed that last for four years without breaking down. They also have added strength and an infrared inhibitor that can reduce heat loss from the greenhouse by up to 20 percent on a clear night. Antidrip surfaces reduce the formation of droplets from moisture condensation on the plastic film surface. Woven polyethylene plastic film—sometimes labeled "rip stop"—provides heavy-duty strength that resists tears.

Although several thicknesses of plastic film are available, the 6-mil thickness is the standard for most applications. It is available in many widths up to 50 feet and in standard lengths of 50 and 100 feet. At 10 to 15 cents per square foot, you can cover a hobby greenhouse for a modest cost.

If attached properly, plastic film will take high winds and heavy snow. Aluminum extrusions nailed to the baseboard and end walls of the greenhouse allow quick attachment and removal. You can also use wood furring strips; double-headed nails will allow for easy removal. Cushion all sharp edges with foam insulation tape to prevent damage from punctures.

Choose a wind-free morning when the temperature is at least 50 degrees F to install the plastic. The easiest way to get the material over the greenhouse is to roll it out along the side of the greenhouse and cut the sheet to length, allowing at least 1 foot extra on each end. Attach a couple of ropes to the leading edge of the plastic and throw the free ends over the ridge. Then pull the plastic sheet over the roof and attach it on all edges. Nail lath or furring strips around openings for windows, vents, and doors, then cut away the plastic.

To conserve winter heat, a double layer should be used. A second sheet can be attached to the inside of the frame with lath or clips. It can also be placed over the top after 2×2 wood spacers are nailed over the first layer. Furring strips hold the second layer in place. Using a double layer of plastic film can reduce heat loss by as much as 35 percent.

Most greenhouse suppliers carry a wide selection of aluminum and galvanized steel framing, glazing materials and attachments, and equipment to outfit the greenhouse.

4-oz. greenhouse-grade fiberglass

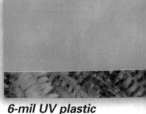

6-mil UV plastic film (poly)

6mm double-wall polycarbonate

8mm triple-wall polycarbonate

Corrugated polycarbonate, clear

Corrugated polycarbonate, matte

COMPARISON OF COMMON GLAZING MATERIALS

Material	Visible Light Transmission	Heat Loss	Estimated Life
Glass			
Single/clear/float or tempered	90%	High	25+ years
Double/clear/tempered	82%	Medium	25+ years
Double/clear/tempered/low-E	78%	Low	25+ years
Double/clear/tempered/heat mirror	56%	Low	25+ years
Double/bronze/heat mirror	40%	Low	25+ years
Rigid plastic			
Single polycarbonate/clear	90%	High	10+ years
Single fiberglass/clear	89%	High	10+ years
Double acrylic/clear	86%	Medium	20+ years
Double polycarbonate/clear	83%	Medium	15+ years
Triple polycarbonate/clear	78%	High	15+ years
Plastic film			
Single/agricultural-grade/clear	87%	High	9 months
Single/greenhouse-grade/clear	87%	High	4 years
Double/greenhouse-grade/clear	78%	Medium	4 years

Source: Adapted from Aldrich & Bartok, Greenhouse Engineering, NRAES-33, 1994.

HEATING AND INSULATION

Rigid insulation, usually made of polyurethane or polystyrene, is the best material for insulating framed knee walls. Fiberglass batting absorbs and holds too much moisture.

Providing heat for your greenhouse all winter long can be expensive if you live in a cold climate. Heat loss through the glazing can be as much as 10 times what is lost through an insulated house wall. There are, however, methods and materials that can be used to reduce the expense of heating.

INSULATION AND ENERGY CONSERVATION

Double or triple glazing can reduce heat loss significantly. Double glazing will reduce heat loss about 30 percent over single glazing. Triple glazing will cut the heat loss in half. Although initially costly, the extra glazing will pay for itself in only a year or two if you heat the greenhouse all winter.

Insulating sidewalls and end walls up to the height of the bench can also reduce heat loss. Polystyrene or polyurethane insulation board works well for this. It can be tacked or clipped to the frame for the winter and removed

Greenhouse bubble insulation can reduce heating costs up to 45 percent. It can last up to four years when used on interior walls.

during the summer. Bags of straw or dry leaves placed along the outside wall of the greenhouse will have the same effect.

A thermal blanket can provide effective insulation. Thermal blankets are insulating materials installed inside the greenhouse on tracks or cables. The blankets are drawn at night like shades to insulate the glazed area and retracted in the morning to let in sunlight.

Although reducing the night-time temperature by 5 degrees F can reduce the heating bill by 10 percent to 20 percent in northern climates, it is important not to exceed any given plant's minimum acceptable temperature.

Keeping the growing area full of plants helps to justify the cost of winter heating. If you are not making good use of the space in the greenhouse, close it down during the coldest part of the winter. You could move the plants into the basement or a spare room and grow them under fluorescent lights.

Landscaping can help insulate the greenhouse. Plant low-growing shrubs around the foundation, or plant a windbreak to help deflect the wind from the structure.

Water while the sun is high to avoid leaving cold, wet surfaces at nightfall.

HEATER SIZE

How much heat your greenhouse will need depends on three factors: size, covering material, and climate. Heat loss is measured in Btus. A Btu is a measure of heat, and by definition 1 Btu equals the amount of energy required to raise 1 pound of water 1 degree F. It takes 8.3 Btus to raise 1 gallon of water 1 degree F. An approximate heater output for your greenhouse should be equal to the heat loss calculated with this formula: $SA \times DR \times IF = HEAT\ LOSS$.

In the above equation, SA represents the total *surface area* to be heated. To determine SA, multiply the length times the height of each wall and roof section (not the floor). Measurements should be in feet. Added together, the total square footage is the SA. The second factor, DR, is the *degree rise* your heater must overcome. It is the difference between the coldest outdoor temperature during the last few years (degrees F) and the night-time temperature you want to maintain in the greenhouse. If you want a minimum of 55 degrees F at night and the lowest expected temperature outside is 15 degrees, then the DR is 40 degrees F. The covering and wind conditions determine the IF, or *insulating factor*, as provided in the following chart:

TEMPERATURE AND PLANT GROWTH

Approximate minimum night-time temperatures for some plants.

45 degrees F	50 degrees F	55 degrees F	60 degrees F
Broccoli	Alstroemeria	Celosia	Achimenes
Brussels sprouts	Antirrhinum	Centaurea	Alternanthera
Cabbage	Citrus	Cypripedium	Begonia
Calceolaria	Cyclamen	Delphinium	Bromeliad
Calendula	Cymbidium	Exacum	Cattleya
Cauliflower	Dendrobium	Fuchsia	Chrysanthemum
Chard	Dianthus	Gerbera	Coleus
Chives	Freesia	Hyacinthus	Cosmos
Endive	Heuchera	Iris (forcing)	Cucumber
Lettuce	Lupinus	Paphiopedilum	Dahlia
Parsley	New Zealand	Pelargonium	Gardenia
Primula	Spinach	Petunia	Kalanchoe
Radish	Squash	Tropaeolum	Rose
Spinach	Streptocarpus	Zantedeschia	Tomato

Adapted from Ohio Research & Development Center Special Circular 104, 1980.

INSULATING FACTOR

Covering	Calm	Windy
Single-layer glass, polycarbonate, fiberglass, or plastic film	1.2	1.4
Double-layer glass, plastic film, polycarbonate, or acrylic sheets	0.8	1.0
Triple-wall polycarbonate	0.6	0.8

Multiply SA × DR × IF to find the heat loss per hour from your greenhouse. When shopping for a heater, look for a Btu output rating that is at least equal to this value.

Example: What size heater is needed for the 10 × 12-foot slant-sided barn-style greenhouse shown on page 44 if it is covered with double-wall polycarbonate and you want to maintain 60 degrees F inside when the minimum temperature is 0 degrees F outside?

Heat loss = SA × DR × IF − 350 sq. ft. × 60 × 0.8 = 16,800 Btu/hr.

HEATING SYSTEMS

Several types of heating units can be used in home greenhouses. Some transfer heat by hot water; others heat the air directly. If you are building an attached greenhouse, you may want to explore the possibility of connecting to the home heating system. Due to the safety hazards, all fuel-fired heating systems require a building permit and should be installed by a licensed heating contractor.

The fuel that you select can have a significant effect on your heating bill. Generally, natural gas is the least expensive. Propane, kerosene, and electricity are other choices. Fuel oil is low in cost, but the smallest units available are too large for a hobby greenhouse under 1,000 square feet of floor area in a cold climate.

The cost of fuel is frequently compared on a dollars per million Btu basis ($/MBtu). The following formulas assume a heater efficiency of 75 percent except for electricity, which is 100 percent.

COST OF FUEL

Natural gas	$/MBtu = $/therm × 13.3
Propane	$/MBtu = $/gallon × 14
Kerosene	$/MBtu = $/gallon × 9.5
Electricity	$/MBtu = $/kWhr × 293

GAS HEATERS

Through-the-wall gas heaters are low-cost, floor-mounted units that exhaust the flue gases through a vent that extends through the sidewall of the greenhouse. Makeup air (the air needed for combustion) is brought into the greenhouse through the outside wall of the same pipe. A pilot light operates continuously, and the thermostat on the outside of the heater turns on the gas valve when heat is needed. A safety shutoff valve is also included. A unit that has an integral fan is desirable, because it circulates the heat, reducing cold spots. There are units available that will work without electricity. They use a mechanical thermostat to turn on the gas.

Unit heaters are usually suspended overhead to allow more growing space and aid in heat distribution. Unit heaters have built-in fans. A valve controls the gas flow and a pilot light or ignition system provides the spark. Flue gases, some of which can be toxic, are vented through a pipe out the end wall.

The vent on this gas heater removes harmful gases such as sulfur dioxide, ethylene, and carbon monoxide.

TIPS TO SAVE ENERGY

■ Add a layer of clear plastic film to the inside of your greenhouse, providing a dead air space between the permanent cover and the insulating layer.

■ Keep the greenhouse cool at night, around 50 degrees F. If you have tender seedlings or germination flats to protect, make a smaller heated chamber to enclose them on the greenhouse bench.

■ Landscape to insulate. Plant low-growing shrubs around the greenhouse foundation, or locate the house about 50 feet from a windbreak of trees or a structure.

■ Keep the greenhouse covering clean. Dirty surfaces mean less light and heat inside.

■ Paint frames, doors, and greenhouse benches white to reflect more sunlight for a warmer growing space.

■ Use concrete for floors, walls, and paths in the greenhouse to absorb heat, which will be released after dark.

■ Water while the sun is high so that cold, wet surfaces can dry out and warm up before nightfall.

■ Make room for a solar heat sink to capture and store heat in the greenhouse.

HEATING AND INSULATION
continued

This electric greenhouse heater has a self-contained fan and thermostat. An electric heater can be a good choice in mild climates where only occasional supplemental heat is needed; it is costly to operate over long periods.

A gas-fired hot water heater can be set up to provide hot water for heating and watering plants. The water temperature in the tank is controlled by a thermostat that activates the gas valve. The hot water is circulated through fin radiators around the perimeter of the greenhouse near the floor. A circulating pump, controlled by a thermostat, activates the pump when the temperature in the greenhouse drops. Hot water for plant watering can be tempered to about 90 degrees F with a mixing valve.

These heating units can be fitted to burn either natural gas or propane. The fuel has to be specified when the unit is ordered. Nonvented heaters should not be used to heat greenhouses. The flue gases given off contain a number of pollutants, including sulfur dioxide, carbon monoxide, and ethylene. These can be toxic to both plants and humans.

KEROSENE HEATERS

Small kerosene heaters with a heat output up to 35,000 Btu/hr are available from several manufacturers. Although some growers have had success with nonvented heaters using the 1-K grade of kerosene, it is best to purchase a heater that can be vented to the outdoors. Most of these heaters do not have a thermostat, so control is limited. The setting you select before you retire in the evening has to be correct to keep the greenhouse warm all night. Portable kerosene heaters work well as an emergency source of heat. Their use over an extended time may cause plant injury due to fumes released by combustion.

Right: A heating and cooling system controller monitors the temperature in the greenhouse and activates different pieces of equipment when necessary.

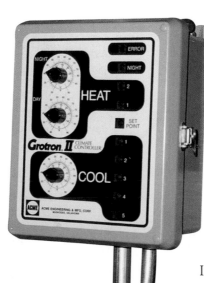

EXTENSION OF THE HOME HEATING SYSTEM

This may be an option if you are building an attached greenhouse or one that will be located close to the home. Have a heating contractor check to see that the existing furnace or boiler in the basement has the extra heat capacity needed. This option is most commonly done with a hot water boiler system. An additional zone with circulating pump, piping, radiators, and thermostat is needed. The pump located on the boiler is activated by the thermostat in the greenhouse. When heat is called for, the pump circulates hot water through the piping and radiators until the thermostat is satisfied. Piping between the greenhouse and the boiler should be insulated to reduce heat loss.

ELECTRIC HEATERS

An electric heater may be a good choice in a mild climate where there are only a few cool nights. It also may work well if you use your greenhouse only in spring to grow transplants for the garden. Utility heaters with an integral thermostat and fan are available in many sizes. Locating one near the end of the greenhouse under a bench will give a circular air pattern and fairly uniform temperature.

Infrared heaters that provide heat similar to the sun work well if mounted overhead in the ridge of the greenhouse. Research has shown that this type of heater saves about 25 percent of electricity costs over a utility heater.

Electric supply has to be adequate to provide the amperage needed. Generally, a 240-volt electric circuit is required.

CONTROLS

Mechanical thermostats are the standard device used to control heating and cooling systems. The best thermostats contain a coil filled with fluid that expands when heated, activating a switch that turns the electricity to the heater or fan on or off. Most mechanical thermostats have a differential of 4 to 6 degrees F between when the switch opens or closes. One thermostat is needed for each device that needs to be controlled.

The electronic thermostat, although more expensive, is much more accurate, having a differential of only 2 degrees F. It also has additional features such as remote sensing, digital temperature display, and day-night operations.

For better control and integration of both the heating and cooling systems, a controller can be used. It monitors conditions in the greenhouse and creates output signals that activate different pieces of equipment. The program board in the controller prevents the heating and cooling systems from operating simultaneously. Additional units that control lighting, misting, and irrigation are available from some manufacturers. These can be connected to a personal computer so that conditions in the greenhouse can be viewed and changed from within the home or office.

SOLAR HEAT

Every gardener uses solar energy every day. Your task is to find ways to store the heat from the daytime until it is needed at night. Heat arrives from the sun in short waves that strike and heat objects in the greenhouse. A south-facing structure with sloped glazing will pick up the most heat energy. Inside the greenhouse, the heated objects radiate warmth in the form of long waves that do not easily escape through the glazing.

Water in barrels painted flat black is one of the best heat sinks. A 55-gallon drum of water heated to 70 degrees F during the day will have about 10,000 Btus of usable heat that can be given back to the greenhouse at night. Several barrels located under the benches in the back of the greenhouse can store enough to supply most of the heat needs on a mild night and can supplement the heating system on a cold night.

Rocks (½ to 1½ inches in diameter), brick, concrete blocks, and a concrete floor store about one-third the quantity of heat on a volume basis compared to drums of water. Insulation under these materials is important to reduce the escape of heat from conduction.

A third class of heat-storage materials includes Glauber's salt and calcium chloride hexahydrate. They are normally contained in plastic or stainless steel tubes stored against the back wall of the greenhouse. These materials change from a solid to a liquid at about 85 degrees F and store considerable heat in this phase change. The heat is released at night as the greenhouse cools.

Installing a few barrels or boxes of rocks can provide some free heat and moderate the temperature in the greenhouse. This source of passive solar doesn't cost much and has a good return. Active solar systems with their associated collectors, pumps, piping, and controls are expensive and would never produce a return on your investment. They are not used for hobby greenhouse heating.

In this angled-wall greenhouse, brick walkways and dark blue barrels filled with water act as solar heat sinks to absorb and slowly emit heat from the sun.

Stainless-steel tubes filled with Glauber's salt or calcium chloride hexahydrate are highly efficient passive solar heat devices that use minimal space.

The sun's warmth is absorbed and held in a thermal-mass heat sink during the day. At night, this heat radiates out and keeps the greenhouse warm.

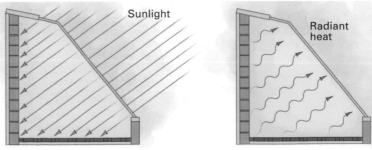

Sunlight

Radiant heat

COOLING

Vents in this greenhouse roof lower the inside temperature by 5 degrees F in a few minutes. White shade cloth reduces heat and light.

Install louvered sidewall and floor-level vents for greater air exchange and temperature moderation.

To prevent excessive heat from drying out your plants and sun-scorching the leaves, your tools are shading, ventilation, fans, and evaporative cooling. High temperatures also reduce flower size, weaken stems, and cause bud abortion.

SHADING

The best way to prevent excessive temperatures in the greenhouse is to reduce the amount of sun's rays that enter through the glazing. This can be done with shade cloth, retractable blinds, or a sprayed-on shade compound.

Shade cloth is woven or knitted from such materials as polypropylene, saran, polyethylene, or polyester. They are lightweight and come in several degrees of shade, from 5 percent to 95 percent. For most crops a 40 percent to 60 percent shade is the best choice. Purchase shade cloth with grommets for easy attachment in a size that will cover the roof area.

In late spring or early summer, install the cloth by tossing it over the roof and securing it, usually with nylon cord or tie-downs that are fastened to screws or hooks in the greenhouse frame. If your greenhouse has roof vents, the shade cloth should be put on in two sections so that the cloth does not cover the vents. If you have fan ventilation, the shade cloth can cover the whole roof.

Shade cloth can be placed inside the greenhouse against the glazing to reduce the direct sunlight on sensitive plants. It does not reduce the temperature within the greenhouse, so the warm air will have to be vented out.

External retractable blinds are available for some kit greenhouses. They fasten to the ridge of the greenhouse and easily roll up or down. Blinds can be made of wooden slats, bamboo, or aluminum. The advantage of this system is that on cloudy days, the blinds can be rolled up, letting in more sunlight.

Shade compounds are materials that are brushed, rolled, or sprayed onto the glazing. Frequently a light coat is applied in late spring, with one or more additional applications during the summer. When fall sets in, most of the shading has worn off. Any remaining material should be removed with a shade compound cleaner before winter.

VENTS

Natural ventilation systems operate on two principles: First, as cool air near the floor is heated, it gets lighter and rises. It escapes out the roof vents and is replaced by cool air that enters through side vents. Second, heat is removed by wind currents that create a vacuum as they pass over the vents.

For vents to be effective, the total vent area should be 20 percent to 30 percent of the floor area split equally between the roof and the sidewalls. Roof vents should be located on the leeward side of the roof (the side away from the normal summer wind direction). The most effective sidewall vent will be located on the windward side of the greenhouse to intercept the breezes.

Vents are hinged on one side and open with levers or arms. They can be opened by hand or powered by a crank and gear box, motorized drive, or solenoid motor. Powered systems are controlled with a thermostat that opens the vent to several positions depending on the ventilation needs.

Nonelectric automatic vents are also available. These open from the expansion of a mineral wax enclosed in a cylinder. A warmer temperature expands the wax and pushes a piston out. The force exerted ranges from 15 to 35 pounds, so the size and weight of the vent that this system will operate are limited. The temperature at which the vent opens is adjustable within a limited range.

CALCULATING FAN NEEDS

To maintain comfortable conditions for your plants, a fan must move large volumes of air in a short period of time. For example, when temperatures in the greenhouse rise above 80 degrees with near-saturation humidity levels, the fan should be powerful enough to change the air about 80 times per hour. Check the fan's capacity ratings at each speed level. If only the highest speed will move your air volume adequately, choose a fan with greater power. In large greenhouses you may need more than one fan.

FANS

Exhaust fans provide better temperature control than vents. A typical system consists of an exhaust fan located in one end wall, an intake louver on the opposite end wall, and a thermostat located in the middle of the greenhouse over the bench at plant height.

Fan size for a greenhouse can be computed by multiplying the floor area in square feet × 12. This value is the output of the fan needed, measured in cubic feet per minute (cfm). For example, a 100-square-foot greenhouse would need a fan having a capacity of 1,200 cfm (100 × 12 = 1,200 cfm). This capacity is measured at $\frac{1}{8}$-inch static pressure (sp). A greenhouse supplier can furnish a fan with a capacity nearest the calculated value; in this case, a 12-inch-diameter fan will do.

For best results the intake louver should be motorized so that it opens when the fan activates. It should be one standard size larger than the fan diameter.

If possible, buy a fan with a two-speed motor—low speed when only a little air is needed, and high speed for warm weather. A two-stage thermostat is required to control the fan.

The fan and intake louver are best located at bench height in the end walls. This circulates the cooling through the plant canopy. If the door to the greenhouse is located on the fan end, be sure that it remains closed when the fan is on; otherwise the air will not circulate properly.

EVAPORATIVE COOLING

Evaporative cooling uses greenhouse heat to evaporate water from leaves and other wet surfaces. This absorbs large quantities of heat in the change of phase from liquid to vapor. With evaporative cooling, the temperature in a greenhouse can be as much as 20 degrees F cooler than outside.

The simplest way to cool a greenhouse is to hose down the floor. Evaporation from the floor is slow, and it needs to be wet frequently, so this is not very effective.

The swamp cooler is the most common way of cooling a home greenhouse by evaporation. The cooler is mounted on a concrete pad next to the greenhouse. Its metal enclosure contains a blower and either cellulose pads and a water pump or a polyester belt that rotates in a pan of water. The dry outside air that is drawn through the pads or belt picks up moisture before it is blown into the greenhouse. This moist air picks up the heat in the greenhouse and then is exhausted through the vents or louvers. A filter may be needed on the water supply to remove particulate matter that could clog the pad. An algicide may also be needed to control algae growth.

To size the cooler, multiply the length of your greenhouse by the width; for a lean-to greenhouse add one-quarter of the area of the wall to which it is attached. Then multiply by 12 to get the blower size in cfm of the unit. Swamp coolers are usually rated by blower size.

Larger greenhouses use a fan and pad system for evaporative cooling. This works on the same principle as the swamp cooler in that it adds moisture to the air.

Exhaust fans provide more efficient cooling than vents alone. The fan is usually located at bench height in one end wall, with an intake louver directly opposite in the other end wall.

Appropriate for large greenhouses, a fan-pad cooler uses an exhaust fan to pull air into the greenhouse through a moist pad.

FAN-PAD COOLER

Detail of PVC pipe and sheet metal strip

Screws and large washers hold the sandwich of wire mesh to the 2×4 frame.

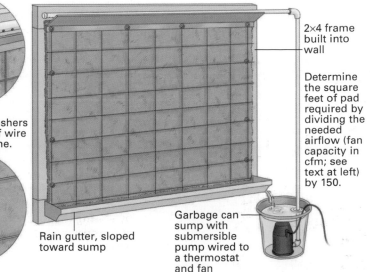

Perforated PVC pipe clamped to a 2×4 frame above a sheet metal strip that directs water onto a pad made of bonded plastic fiber coated with absorbent cellular foam

2×4 frame built into wall

Determine the square feet of pad required by dividing the needed airflow (fan capacity in cfm; see text at left) by 150.

Rain gutter, sloped toward sump

Garbage can sump with submersible pump wired to a thermostat and fan

GREENHOUSE PLANS

The plans in this chapter present a variety of greenhouse components that have stood the test of time. The plans are presented as practical guides that can be customized and combined according to your gardening needs, construction skills, location, and budget.

Each plan consists of three parts: a schematic drawing, a discussion, and a photograph. Once you have studied all the plans, use graph paper to draw floor plans and elevations to create a plan that's right for you.

THE PLAN FOR YOUR SITE

As you examine these plans, you will see that most of the greenhouses can be built with a simple wooden base or a more substantial concrete foundation. All can be covered with flexible plastic film or rigid plastic panels; a few may be covered with glass. Refer to "Construction Basics," starting on page 14, for more information on foundations and materials.

If you live where the weather is windy or harsh, build on a concrete or wooden post foundation and use lumber rather than plastic pipe for the frame. No matter what the frame weighs, it will last longer if it is built on a concrete foundation than if it is simply anchored to the ground.

Solar greenhouses such as the one on pages 50 and 51 depend on a sunny climate to operate efficiently. If your site doesn't receive full sun most of the year, plan to include a heat sink and other passive solar features.

If you live where winters are mild enough to grow parsley outdoors during most years, you may opt for a covering of flexible plastic film, perhaps just a single layer of 6-mil thickness. At the other end of the climate spectrum, a cold, windy winter can make most greenhouses impractical, but attached structures and sun pits can better withstand the harsh conditions.

This chapter leads you through the process of building a greenhouse and teaches you a bit about construction in general at the same time. Terms used are clearly defined either in the text or in separate definition boxes, and directions are clear for the do-it-yourselfer.

Reading carefully through all the plans will help you understand any one of them. Each plan details a greenhouse feature or construction technique that is challenging or different from the others, and you can use much of the information interchangeably.

TOOLS FOR THE TASKS

A handy do-it-yourselfer can build any of these greenhouses with basic hand tools: saw, hammer, screwdriver, chisel, rasp, sawhorses, tape measure, square, level, chalk line, mortar trowel, caulking gun, and safety glasses. In addition, you may need a ladder, wheelbarrow, shovel, and posthole digger. Work will go faster with a power saw, a nail or staple gun, and a battery-operated power drill with bits to attach frame members and covers. Equipment such as a cement mixer or backhoe can be rented to aid in some projects.

THE MATERIALS LISTS

Each greenhouse plan has a materials list that includes the lumber, supplies, and tools needed. Used as a guide to provide a shorthand look at what you'll be working with, the list will help in your planning. For accuracy and to be sure you know how the pieces will fit together, make your own estimates using the suggestions provided. Copy the list, figure the amount of lumber you'll need, and estimate your costs.

Unless stated otherwise, the materials used have the following characteristics: all nails are galvanized; all corrugated materials are attached with corrugated molding and aluminum nails with flexible washers; flexible plastics are UV treated and attached with furring strips or aluminum extrusions; rigid plastics are covered by a ridgecap at the roof peak.

COLD FRAMES AND HOTBEDS

A cold frame and a hotbed are each minigreenhouses that can help extend the growing season. A cold frame is a bottomless box with a slanted, transparent top used to protect tender plants from freezing. A hotbed has a heat source inside, such as a layer of fresh manure or an electric heat cable. The latter will use about 1 to 2 kilowatts per day. Cold frames and hotbeds are built essentially the same way and are easy to construct.

To trap the sun, the cold frame needs a cover. Old windows can serve the purpose, and you can build a base box to fit. Or you can build a 1×3 or 1×4 frame around a sheet of rigid plastic, or cover a frame with plastic film. Attach the cover to the box with hinges.

For a 4-foot-square box, use three 1×12 (or 2×12) boards, each 8 feet long. Cut as shown in the diagram below. Use galvanized deck screws, angle irons, and brackets to attach the pieces together. Check that the box is level, then put in 6 inches of well-drained soil mix.

The hotbed is built the same way, but its construction starts with a shovel. Dig a pit slightly smaller than 4 feet square, and deep enough to suit your heat source: 10 inches for manure, 6 inches for a heating cable. If you are using manure, shovel in a layer of chicken or horse manure after the box is in place. Lay a piece of window screen on top of the manure, then add a layer of soil mix.

If you are using heating cable, install it in a serpentine pattern at the bottom of the pit, with its cord running to the outside to connect with a power source. Connect it to a thermostat with a remote sensor placed in the soil to prevent overheating. Electricity can come from an outdoor extension cord plugged into a receptacle in the garage or on the back porch. Spread 6 inches of sand on top of the cable and the soil mix on top of that.

Choose a method to vent the box daily. Simply lift off the cover and set it aside; if it is hinged, prop it open with a notched stick. Or let an automatic thermal vent opener do the work for you (see page 28).

Locate your cold frame or hotbed so its slanted top faces the sun for as many hours a day as possible. You can use the frame all summer by changing to a screen cover that allows airflow but excludes insects.

COLD FRAME / HOTBED CONSTRUCTION

Angle iron   Hinges
Glass or plastic cover
Angle bracket
Soil mix
Screen
Manure

Flat corner brace
Mending plate

4'5⅝"

4'   4'

1×12 boards cut for base. Or use 2×12s, which cost more but are sturdier and longer-lasting.

4'   4'

Top of back
Diagonals

Diagonals and back are attached to top of 1×12 base with angle irons and brackets.

MATERIALS LIST

LUMBER: Use pressure-treated wood or redwood. Box: 3 1×12s, 8 ft. Cover: 2 1×3s, 12 ft. (for poly cover add 2 lath strips, 8 ft.)

COVERING: Rigid plastic or flexible plastic film, 4×4

SUPPLIES: Nails and screws, hinges, 4 angle irons, 4 angle brackets, 4 flat corner braces, 2 mending plates, screening or wire mesh

TOOLS: Tape measure, hammer, saw, screwdriver, carpenter's square, level, drill and bits, shovel

HOOP GREENHOUSE

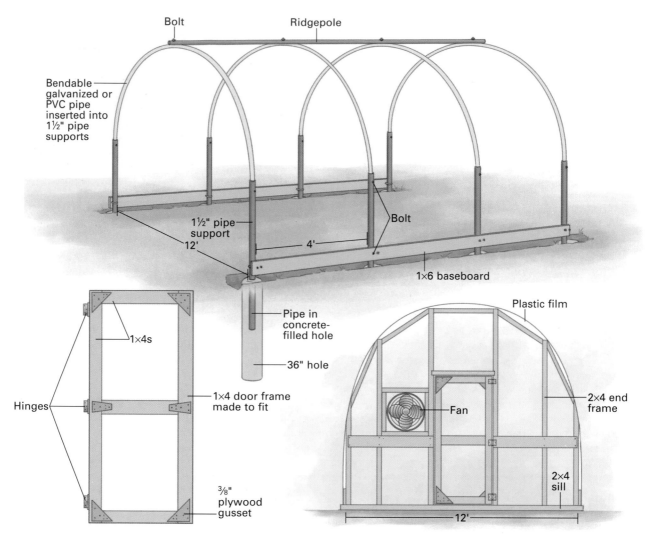

Bolt

Ridgepole

Bendable galvanized or PVC pipe inserted into 1½" pipe supports

1½" pipe support

Bolt

12'

4'

1×6 baseboard

Pipe in concrete-filled hole

36" hole

1×4s

Hinges

1×4 door frame made to fit

⅜" plywood gusset

Plastic film

Fan

2×4 end frame

2×4 sill

12'

This hoop structure is one of the simplest greenhouses to build. Its frame is constructed from plastic or metal pipe hoops and covered with plastic film. This lightweight construction, however, cannot withstand snow or strong winds. Hoops are available ready-made from greenhouse suppliers, or you may fabricate your own from materials available at a home center. Long lengths of PVC pipe can be bent and attached to the base by hand; a local metalwork shop can bend galvanized pipe into shape for you.

Pick a sunny, level site and square up a perimeter 12 feet wide and as long as you wish in 4-foot increments. Dig a trench along the two long sides of the greenhouse, 4 to 5 inches wide and deep. Mark spots 4 feet apart on center along each side.

The foundation is formed by driving metal pipe or tubing into the ground. These ground posts are typically 4 to 6 feet long. A minimum of 30 inches should be driven into the ground, leaving 1 to 4 feet exposed above ground, depending on how tall you want the center height of your greenhouse to be. The taller the structure, the longer the pipe.

At each marked spot, drive a post into the ground using a hammer, maul, or post driver. Place a wood cap over the top of the post to prevent damage when it is being hammered.

For more permanent installation, dig postholes 6 inches wide and 3 to 4 feet deep (or about 6 inches below the frost line). Fill the holes with concrete. Before it sets, sink a piece of 1½-inch rigid PVC or galvanized pipe 2 to 3 feet into the mix. Use a level to make sure each foundation pipe is set straight up and down. (When shopping for ground posts and hoops, be sure the hoop material you choose fits tightly inside the posts.)

Once the posts are set, bolt 1×6 pressure-treated baseboards to the outside of the posts, extending several inches below grade into the trench. Drill holes through the boards and pipes to attach them with bolts and nuts. You may also add insulation board to the inside of the post line in the same way.

Next insert the pipe hoops into the foundation pipes. Put all the hoops in place, then glue or bolt the joints where the hoops are inserted into the ground posts. For added stability, bolt a piece of pipe or wood running the length of the structure along the top of the hoops as a ridgepole.

Build a 1×4 door frame (see illustration) to accommodate a standard storm door (6 feet 8 inches high, with a width of 30, 32, or 36 inches). Or make a door to fit from 2×2s with one cross brace at the center. Triangular plywood gussets at each corner add strength. The door should swing out to save interior space, and it should be hinged so it does not open into the prevailing wind.

For best ventilation, put a door in each end, or plan for a large vent opening in the wall opposite the door. Attach the end-wall frame to the hoop on each end with bolts or U-shaped pipe clamps.

Cover the end walls of the house with flexible plastic film. Use as few pieces as possible for strength. Secure the plastic by nailing pieces of wooden lath over the plastic into the 2×4 frame. At the hoop, wrap the plastic around the pipe and secure it with tape for now.

To cover the roof with plastic film, find a friend or two to help. Choose a windless day to work. Unroll the plastic and cut a sheet long enough to cover the greenhouse with at least 1 foot extra on each side. Attach the film to the baseboard on one side of the greenhouse with lath. Tie strong ropes through holes in the other end of the film, and pull the sheet up and over the hoops. If more than one piece of film is needed to cover the frame, overlap the pieces by 6 inches or more.

MATERIALS LIST

LUMBER:
Baseboards: 2 1×6s, 12 ft. long
End frames: 16 2×4s, 10 ft.; 4 2×4s, 12 ft.; 20 lath strips, 10 ft.
Ground posts: 8 pieces 1½-inch galvanized (or PVC) pipe, 8 ft.
Hoops: 8 pieces flexible PVC or galvanized pipe, 10 ft. (with couplings). For ridgepole, use one piece of galvanized pipe or PVC, 12 ft.
Door: 2 1×4s, 8 ft.; 2 1×4s, 6 ft.; ⅜-inch plywood, 4×4 sheet
COVERING: 8-mil UV-protected plastic film to cover 30×12-ft. roof area plus approx. 210 sq. ft. ends (add for overlapping)
SUPPLIES: Pipe clamps, nails and screws, ¼-inch bolts and nuts, pipe glue, PVC pipe couplings, door hinges and handle, 10 bags of ready-to-use concrete mix
TOOLS: Tape measure, hammer, saw, power drill and bits, screwdriver, carpenter's square, level, shovel, posthole digger, tub and hoe for mixing concrete

Attach the film to the other baseboard using lath strips. Bury the excess film on each side in the trenches and cover with soil to hold it down. On the ends, fold over the film and attach it to the end wall frames with pieces of wooden lath.

Alternative foundation: A small hoop greenhouse can rest on a foundation made of two 2×4s stacked and nailed together. Bore holes in these foundation boards to hold the hoops. Use stakes or anchors to hold the foundation boards to the ground, as described for the Gothic-arch greenhouse on page 37. Bury the covering outside the frame or attach it with lath at ground level.

Alternative material for hoops: Redwood bender board (a 4- or 6-inch-wide lath strip often used to edge garden beds) lends itself nicely to this construction. Bender boards can be screwed into place on a 2×4 foundation and covered with plastic film.

DEFINING TERMS

GUSSET: A piece of plywood or sheet metal cut to join two framing members together. Gussets are usually placed on the front and/or the back of a joint and require a significant number of nails to make the joint rigid and strong.

Build a hoop greenhouse for its economy and versatility in areas with mild winters and hot summers.

ALTERNATIVE PIPE FOUNDATION

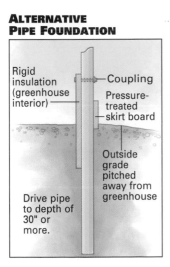

Rigid insulation (greenhouse interior)

Coupling

Pressure-treated skirt board

Outside grade pitched away from greenhouse

Drive pipe to depth of 30" or more.

CLASSIC A-FRAME GREENHOUSE

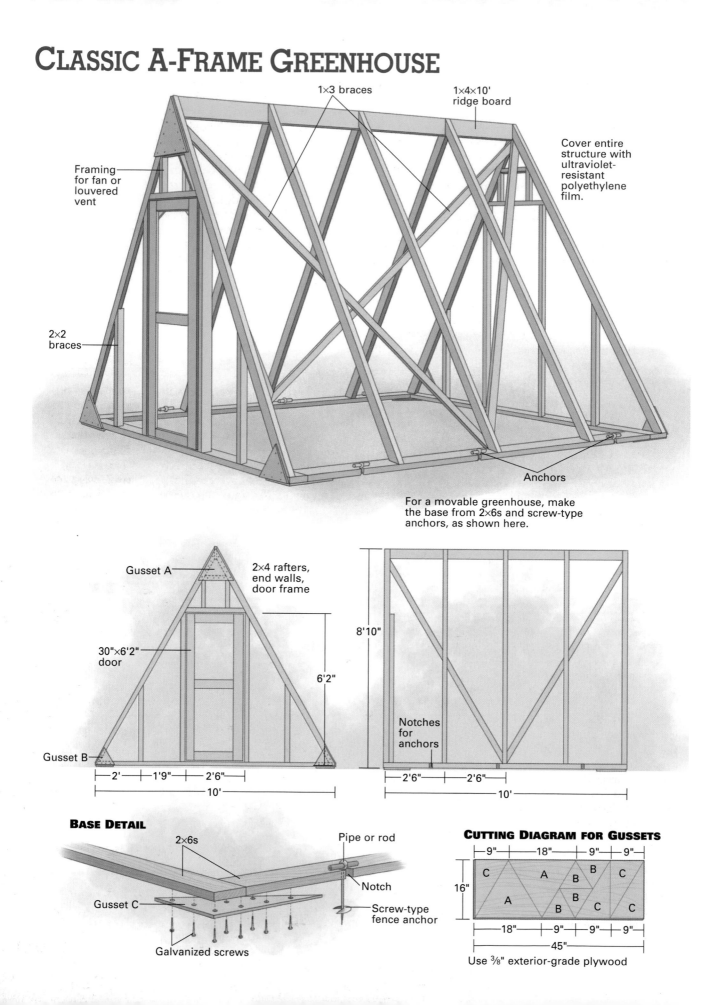

1×3 braces

1×4×10' ridge board

Framing for fan or louvered vent

Cover entire structure with ultraviolet-resistant polyethylene film.

2×2 braces

Anchors

For a movable greenhouse, make the base from 2×6s and screw-type anchors, as shown here.

Gusset A

2×4 rafters, end walls, door frame

30"×6'2" door

6'2"

8'10"

Gusset B

Notches for anchors

2'   1'9"   2'6"

2'6"   2'6"

10'

10'

BASE DETAIL

2×6s

Pipe or rod

Notch

Gusset C

Screw-type fence anchor

Galvanized screws

CUTTING DIAGRAM FOR GUSSETS

9"   18"   9"   9"

C   A   B   C

16"

A   B   C   C

B

18"   9"   9"   9"

45"

Use ⅜" exterior-grade plywood

The chief advantage of an A-frame greenhouse lies in its easy construction. The steep roof sheds snow, rain, and leaves efficiently and makes for easy installation of shade cloth. This model is relatively small and lightweight and could be moved by a few people if necessary. These plans show the A-frame on a 2×6 base set on the ground with anchors, but you could build it on a concrete foundation. Simply attach the rafters and end framing to a 2×6 foundation sill.

Locate the A-frame greenhouse so the ridge runs from east to west for maximum light into the growing space throughout the day. This design uses one door only, but if you live in a moderate or warm climate and need maximum ventilation, add a door or large vent to the other end. Review the information about squaring up on page 14 to establish a workable perimeter.

The greenhouse sits on a 10×10-foot base made of pressure-treated wood. You will need four 2×6s: the end boards are 10 feet long, and the side pieces are cut to 9 feet 1 inch. Assemble them as shown in the detail on the facing page. Reinforce the corners with braces called gussets. Use ⅜-inch exterior plywood to cut gussets as illustrated in the diagram.

Anchor the greenhouse to the ground. This design uses a screw-type fence anchor set into notches cut in the base and held in place with short pieces of pipe or metal bar pushed through the screw eye.

Ten 2×4s, 10 feet long, are needed for the rafters. The 10-foot ridge board and the door are made from 1×4s. Additional bracing can use 1×3 pieces (2×2s for the end walls).

Lay out the end wall frames. Cut one rafter to fit the gusset at the proper angle (about 60 degrees) and use it as the pattern for the other nine rafters. Build each end wall, first nailing the end rafters to the 2×6 base. Use temporary braces to hold the end rafters in place. Nail the 1×4 ridge board between the upper ends of the rafters. Screw on gussets to strengthen the joints.

Nail the other three rafters in place on each sidewall. Check to be sure the frame and rafters are square, then nail the diagonal braces in place across the rafters and remove the temporary braces.

To provide adequate ventilation in this design, frame in a 10-inch-diameter louvered vent opening above the door and the same size opening for a fan at the opposite end of the greenhouse.

This model is covered on the outside with 6-mil flexible plastic sheeting. Secure the plastic to the frame with wood lath strips. In areas where winter temperatures stay below 30 degrees, put another layer of polyethylene inside; 4-mil plastic film is adequate for this purpose. By covering the outside and inside of a 2×4 frame, you create a heat-retaining thermal barrier space.

Simple yet strong, A-frames offer growing space for tall plants and still let in plenty of light below them. This one, with its long wall facing the sun, is used to prepare bedding plants for spring transplanting.

MATERIALS LIST

LUMBER:
Base: 4 2×6s, 10 ft.
Rafters, end walls: 16 2×4s, 10 ft.; 4 2×4s, 12 ft.
Ridge board: 1 1×4, 10 ft.
Braces: 2 2×2s, 6 ft.; 4 1×3s, 12 ft.
Gussets: 4×4 piece ⅜-inch exterior plywood
To attach covering: 20 lath strips, 10 ft.
(Door: see page 32)
COVERING: 6-mil (and 4-mil for lining) plastic film (each to cover approx. 300 sq. ft.)
SUPPLIES: Galvanized nails and wood screws, 6 fence anchors, door hardware, pieces of rebar or pipe for anchors
TOOLS: Hammer, saw, screwdriver, drill and bits, square, level, tape measure

GOTHIC-ARCH GREENHOUSE

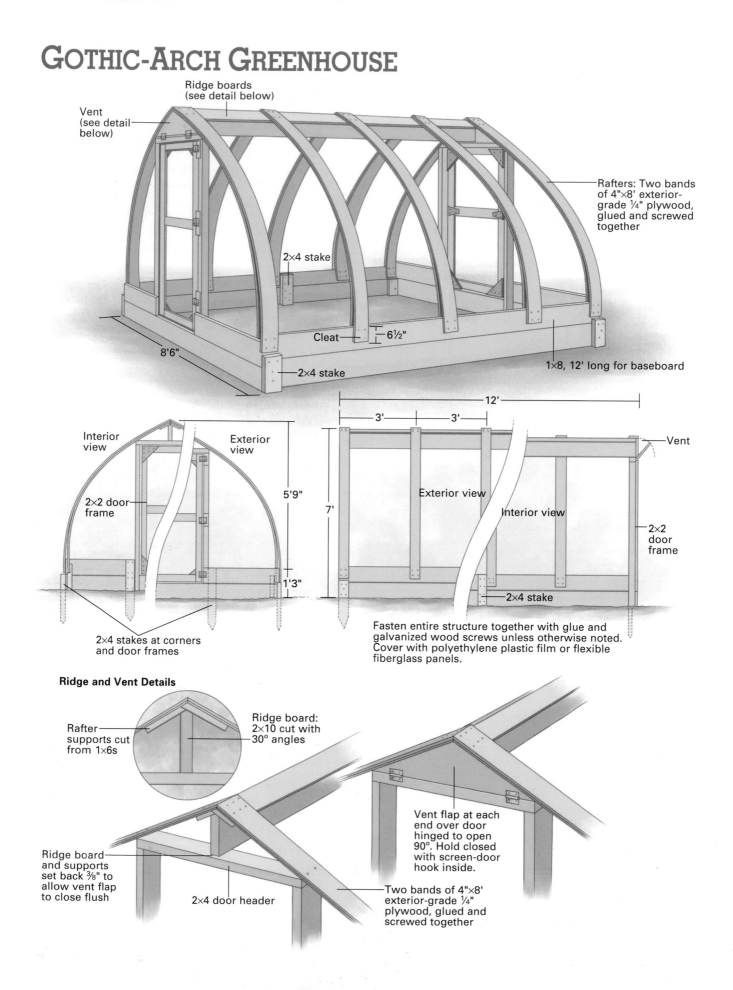

Ridge boards
(see detail below)

Vent
(see detail
below)

Rafters: Two bands
of 4"×8' exterior-
grade ¼" plywood,
glued and screwed
together

2×4 stake

8'6"

Cleat

6½"

2×4 stake

1×8, 12' long for baseboard

Interior
view

Exterior
view

2×2 door
frame

5'9"

1'3"

2×4 stakes at corners
and door frames

12'

3'   3'

7'

Exterior view

Interior view

Vent

2×2
door
frame

2×4 stake

Fasten entire structure together with glue and
galvanized wood screws unless otherwise noted.
Cover with polyethylene plastic film or flexible
fiberglass panels.

Ridge and Vent Details

Rafter
supports cut
from 1×6s

Ridge board:
2×10 cut with
30° angles

Vent flap at each
end over door
hinged to open
90°. Hold closed
with screen-door
hook inside.

Ridge board
and supports
set back ⅜" to
allow vent flap
to close flush

2×4 door header

Two bands of 4"×8'
exterior-grade ¼"
plywood, glued and
screwed together

The Gothic-arch greenhouse offers two options for the builder. Although designed to be portable, this greenhouse could be placed on a concrete foundation for more permanence. It can be covered with plastic film or more durable fiberglass panels.

Using two 1×8s stacked on edge and cleated together, make a foundation frame measuring 12 feet long and 8 feet 6 inches wide. To further stabilize the foundation, drive 2×4 stakes 24 inches into the ground on each side of the door and two on each side of the frame. Fasten the stakes to the frame with galvanized wood screws. Another anchoring method is to drive 24-inch lengths of rebar 18 inches deep and 18 inches apart around the perimeter. Use pipe clamps or J nails to secure the bars to the 1×8s.

For the roof supports, cut 20 strips, each 4 inches wide and 8 feet long, from ¼-inch exterior-grade plywood. For longer life, treat the wood with non-oil-based preservative. Glue and nail or staple the roof supports together in twos, leaving the bottom 8 inches unconnected, creating 10 bands.

The next step is to frame the end walls and the door openings. At each end, frame an opening 2 feet 6 inches wide. Use 2×4 cleats or stakes on either side of the opening to hold the 2×4 frame members.

Cut two lengths of 2×4 to run vertically between the bottom board of the frame and the roof supports. These studs will also hold the door. Allow for a 2×4 door header at the top of the opening. Cut a header and a threshold 2 feet 6 inches wide and nail the door frame into position on the base. Temporary braces will help hold the frame upright and square.

For the ridge board, cut or plane 30-degree bevels on one edge of a 12-foot length of 2×10 (see detail). Trim ¾ inch off the length of the ridge board and toenail it in place on the center of the door headers, set back ⅜ inch from the edge of the headers. To each side of the ridge board, nail a 1×6, 12 feet (minus ¾ inch) long, flush with the angle. This forms the support for the bands of plywood rafters.

Start with an end rafter. Attach the bands to the ridgeline with galvanized wood screws, overhanging the ridge board and supports by ⅜ inch and flush with the end wall frame. Curve the rafter over the door frame and nail it there, then bend it down to the base frame. Place the top flap of the rafter outside the frame and the bottom flap inside. Attach with screws. Complete both ends first, then finish with the middle supports.

The spaces above the greenhouse doors can be used for vents. Cut pieces of ⅜-inch exterior-grade plywood to fit the gable openings above the doors. Attach the vents with hinges so they can be opened, and secure them inside with a hook and eye (see detail).

Complete the greenhouse by covering it with flexible fiberglass panels or plastic film. For more on how to attach panels, see page 46.

DEFINING TERMS

CLEAT: A strip of wood or metal used to strengthen a joint in a frame. Where one piece of a frame butts against the other, a cleat is laid over the joint and nailed or screwed to fasten the pieces together.

The curved walls of the Gothic-arch greenhouse shed heavy snow and rain and let in abundant sunlight.

MATERIALS LIST

LUMBER:
End frame, stakes, cleats: 8 2×4s, 8 ft.
Baseboards: 4 1×8s, 12 ft.; 4 1×8s, 10 ft.
Rafters: ¼-inch plywood, 2 4×8 sheets
Vents: ⅜-inch plywood, 1 4×4 piece
Ridge board: 1 2×10, 12 ft.
Rafter supports: 2 1×6s, 12 ft.
(Door: see page 32)
COVERING: Flexible plastic panels or plastic film (to cover approx. 320 sq. ft.)
SUPPLIES: Galvanized nails and wood screws, rebar, hinges, door handles, screen-door hooks, wood glue
TOOLS: Hammer, saw, drill and bits, staple gun, carpenter's square, level, clamps, chalk line, plumb bob, measuring tape

MODIFIED A-FRAME GREENHOUSE

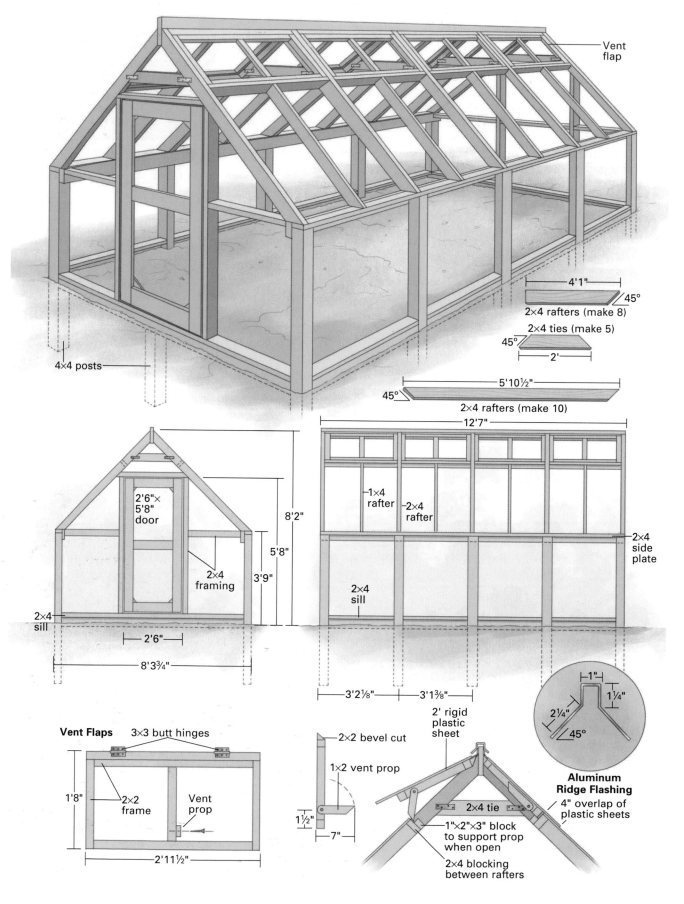

Vent flap

4×4 posts

4'1"
45°
2×4 rafters (make 8)

2×4 ties (make 5)
45°
2'

5'10½"
45°
2×4 rafters (make 10)

2'6"× 5'8" door

2×4 framing

8'2"
5'8"
3'9"

2×4 sill

2'6"

8'3¾"

12'7"

1×4 rafter
2×4 rafter

2×4 side plate

2×4 sill

3'2⅛"
3'1⅜"

Vent Flaps
3×3 butt hinges
2×2 frame
Vent prop
1'8"
2'11½"

2×2 bevel cut
1×2 vent prop
1½"
7"

2' rigid plastic sheet
2×4 tie
1"×2"×3" block to support prop when open
2×4 blocking between rafters

1"
1¼"
2¼"
45°

Aluminum Ridge Flashing
4" overlap of plastic sheets

Developed by Ralph Letters at the University of Connecticut, this greenhouse features a steep A-frame roof for shedding snow easily. Because the A sits on top of a box base framed by 4×4 posts, it has more headroom and usable space inside than a simple A-frame. The continuous line of roof vents provides natural cooling in the summer months.

To build this greenhouse, start by squaring the site and extending strings to mark its exact perimeter (see page 14). This structure's success depends on the careful placement of its post foundation. Sink twelve 4×4 posts about 2 feet in the ground (or 6 inches below the frost line); consult the plan at left for exact positioning. The top of the two posts in the center of each end wall should be cut flush with the bottom of the foot plate. The ten side-wall posts should be set with 3 feet 9 inches remaining above the surface. To get these exact measurements, after sinking the posts use a line level to measure and mark them, then cut the tops at the required height. For the rafters to fit smoothly, each pair of side-wall posts must be set 8 feet 3¾ inches apart measured on the outside.

After the posts are in place, link them with a doubled 2×4 foot plate. Next nail a 2×4 sill on top of the posts. Attach a 2×4 side plate inside the posts and flush with the sill, which will help support the rafter ends.

You will need ten 2×4 rafters, 5 feet 10½ inches long, and eight 2×4 rafters, 4 feet 1 inch long. Cut a 45-degree angle at both ends of the long rafters and a 45-degree angle at the bottom end only of the eight short rafters. To keep cuts consistent, measure the first carefully as a pattern, check its fit, and use it as a template to cut the others just the same.

Frame the door and facing end wall, and use the framing to support the end rafters. Next nail the end rafters to the 1×8 ridge board. Put up the other 2×4 rafters, spaced 3 feet 1⅜ inches on center, centered over the foundation posts. Attach the 1×8 ties to the long rafters.

Use 2×4s to frame the vent openings along the roof ridge. Then center the 1×4 rafters on the blocking and toenail them in. Frame the vents with 2×2s cut according to the illustration to fit between each rafter.

Cover this greenhouse with rigid plastic panels and add an aluminum flashing on the ridge. In cold-winter climates, this frame can be covered with triple-wall plastic panels, which provide better insulation and are much lighter to support than glass.

In cold-winter areas, heating needs can be reduced with an insulated floor. If digging a trenched floor to hold insulation is not practical, build up the floor. Add insulation to the floor, and put a walkable surface such as paving stones or slats on top of it.

WOODEN WALL WEATHERPROOFING

One design option to adapt this greenhouse for cold climates is to change the north end of the box base to an insulated wooden wall. Build the frame as directed, then cover the lower north wall outside with ⅜-inch exterior plywood, then siding or shingles. On the inside, use rigid insulation panels to fill the space, then cover it with ¼-inch exterior plywood and paint it white.

MATERIALS LIST

LUMBER:
Rafters, sill, plates, blocking: 40 2×4s, 8 ft.; 4 2×4s, 10 ft.
Ridge board: 1 2×4, 14 ft.
Rafter ties: 2 2×4s, 6 ft.
Foundation posts: 12 4×4s, 6 ft.
(Door: see page 32)
COVERING: Rigid plastic panels (to cover approx. 380 sq. ft.), extruded metal framing
SUPPLIES: Galvanized nails and wood screws, caulk, weather stripping, paint, hinges, door hardware, wood glue, 8-inch-wide aluminum flashing
TOOLS: Hammer, saw, drill and bits, carpenter's square, level, clamps, chalk line, plumb bob, posthole digger, measuring tape

The steeply sloped roof of this modified A-frame sheds snow, heavy rain, and leaves. The boxy lower frame creates a wide interior that leaves room for storage or growing under the bench.

SUN-PIT GREENHOUSE

Sun-pit greenhouses use the insulation of the ground to provide a moderate environment with little need for supplemental heating. The roof can be framed with wood, as shown, or with heavy-duty extruded metal supports that are glazed with double- or triple-wall polycarbonate panels.

Painting all interior surfaces white will maximize the sunlight.

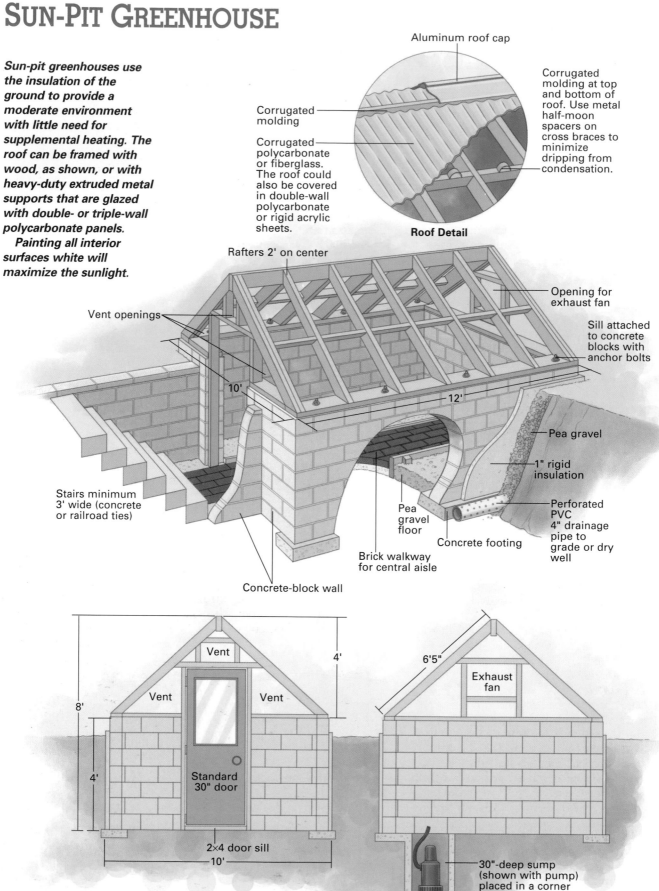

Aluminum roof cap

Corrugated molding

Corrugated polycarbonate or fiberglass. The roof could also be covered in double-wall polycarbonate or rigid acrylic sheets.

Corrugated molding at top and bottom of roof. Use metal half-moon spacers on cross braces to minimize dripping from condensation.

Roof Detail

Rafters 2' on center

Vent openings

Opening for exhaust fan

Sill attached to concrete blocks with anchor bolts

10'

12'

Pea gravel

1" rigid insulation

Stairs minimum 3' wide (concrete or railroad ties)

Pea gravel floor

Concrete footing

Perforated PVC 4" drainage pipe to grade or dry well

Brick walkway for central aisle

Concrete-block wall

Vent

Vent

Vent

4'

8'

4'

Standard 30" door

2×4 door sill

10'

6'5"

Exhaust fan

30"-deep sump (shown with pump) placed in a corner beneath a bench

A sun-heated pit greenhouse, with a foundation sunk below ground and a roof rising from ground level, is reminiscent of a walk-in cold frame. The roof in this design is an A-frame, although rounded and arched styles may be used instead. Seldom seen today, the sun pit deserves more attention for its practicality.

The sun pit requires little or no external heating, especially if you use it as a cool greenhouse. It takes advantage of the natural insulation of the ground and suffers little heat loss through the walls. Its low profile protects it from the wind.

Its main disadvantage is the cost of excavation, because a backhoe is usually needed. The efficient natural insulation can also create difficulties in venting the structure. Accessibility can be a problem, too, because the sun pit is entered by descending several steps. And in heavy rainstorms, water may wash into it.

If ample sunlight and excellent drainage are available on your site, a sun pit may be a good choice. Locate the long wall facing south and make it as long as is practical— at least 12 feet long for a pit 8 feet wide. The pit should be 4 feet deep—thus the likelihood you will want to rent a backhoe.

Once the pit is dug, square the sides until they are vertical, and level the floor. Be sure

the floor is pitched to drain toward the sump location. Around the edge, dig a trench 4 inches deep and 12 inches wide for the footing. Dig a sump 30 inches deep and 18 inches wide to collect irrigation and seepage water. This may be filled with gravel as a dry well, or left open for installation of a sump pump. Dig access for the steps at the end away from prevailing winds, and run water and electrical lines before proceeding with the foundation wall.

Build a concrete-block wall for the pit and retaining walls for the stairs. Place rigid insulation on the outside of the wall, then backfill. Add a 2×4 or 2×6 sill on top of the wall, attached to the wall with anchor bolts.

Finish the floor while you can still get a wheelbarrow into the pit. The ground provides insulation, so a 4-inch layer of pea gravel is all you need. Spread it before you begin to assemble the roof.

For the A-frame roof, start by framing the door and rafters on one end, the gable end rafters and vent opening at the other. This plan shows an 8-foot height from floor to ridge. To find the angle of the end cuts so the rafters fit tightly against the ridge board and the sills, hold one rafter in place at the end, mark it, and use it as a pattern for the other rafters. For a 12-foot-long sun pit, cut 18 2×4 rafters and place them 2 feet on center, doubling the end rafters to provide a nailing surface for the end walls. Place vent openings in each end wall directly under the ridge. For additional ventilation, install a fan and intake louver.

The roof is covered in corrugated fiberglass or polycarbonate. Acrylic sheets or double-wall polycarbonate could be used instead.

DEFINING TERMS

SUMP PUMP: A device that pumps water up; that is, when you install one in an overflow trench (also called a sump), a sump pump moves the irrigation and seepage water up and out of the greenhouse.

MATERIALS LIST

LUMBER:
Batter boards (for foundation and walls): 8 2×4s, 8 ft.; 4 1×4s, 8 ft.
Rafters, framing, blocking: 24 2×4s, 8 ft.
Sill and ridge board: 3 2×6s, 12 ft.; 2 2×6s, 8 ft.
Steps, or landscape timbers to make them
Concrete blocks: approx. 260 stretcher blocks (8×8×16 and half-blocks)
1-inch rigid insulation: 5 4×8 sheets
COVERING:
Corrugated polycarbonate or double-wall polycarbonate (to cover approx. 200 sq. ft.); extruded metal framing
SUPPLIES: Galvanized nails and wood screws, anchor bolts, caulk, string, stakes, weather stripping, staples, paint, hinges, 12-ft. aluminum roof cap or flashing, pea gravel and/or brick for flooring, mortar, rebar, J bolts
TOOLS: Hammer, saw, drill and bits, staple gun, carpenter's square, level, clamps, mortar trowel, chalk line, plumb bob, measuring tape

The initial extra costs of the sun-pit greenhouse can be recouped rapidly by saving on heating costs over the first few seasons of use.

BARN-STYLE GREENHOUSE

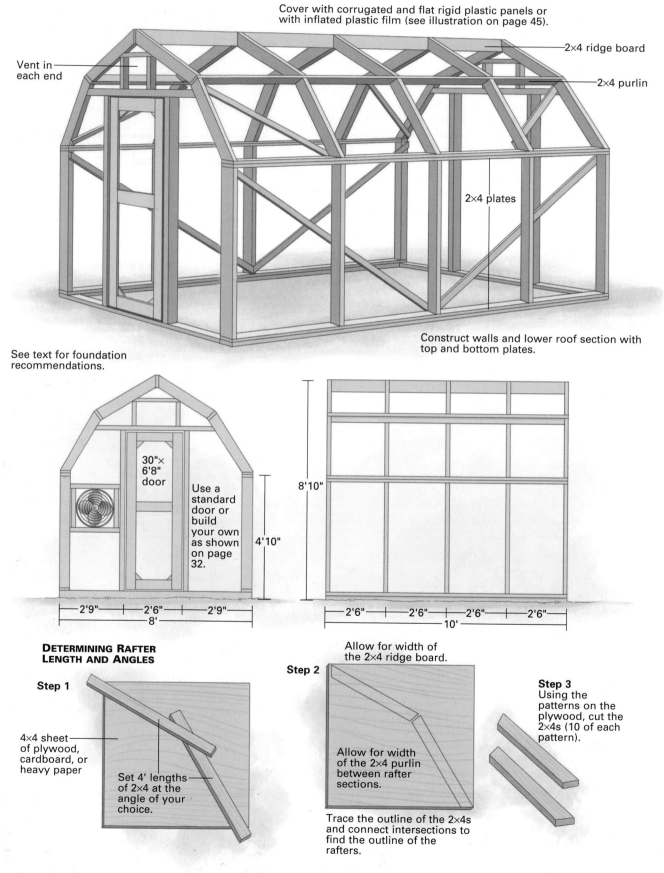

Cover with corrugated and flat rigid plastic panels or with inflated plastic film (see illustration on page 45).

2×4 ridge board

2×4 purlin

Vent in each end

2×4 plates

See text for foundation recommendations.

Construct walls and lower roof section with top and bottom plates.

30"× 6'8" door

Use a standard door or build your own as shown on page 32.

4'10"

8'10"

2'9"   2'6"   2'9"
8'

2'6"   2'6"   2'6"   2'6"
10'

DETERMINING RAFTER LENGTH AND ANGLES

Step 1

4×4 sheet of plywood, cardboard, or heavy paper

Set 4' lengths of 2×4 at the angle of your choice.

Step 2

Allow for width of the 2×4 ridge board.

Allow for width of the 2×4 purlin between rafter sections.

Trace the outline of the 2×4s and connect intersections to find the outline of the rafters.

Step 3
Using the patterns on the plywood, cut the 2×4s (10 of each pattern).

The freestanding barn-style greenhouse is popular with do-it-yourselfers. The roofline resembles that of a classic Midwestern barn; tall and wide, its additional surface area lets in plenty of light, with headroom for specimen plants in the growing area. The design calls for vents in the end walls; if you live in a warm climate, it is easy to add more vents in the sides.

This 8×12-foot design can be built on freestanding 2×6 foundation plates, anchored by wooden or metal stakes, as described in the A-frame greenhouse plan (see page 35). A poured footing or cement-block foundation will give the structure greater permanence and make it less vulnerable to wind damage.

Framing begins with a sill, which will sit on top of the ground board or concrete footing. Once the sill is in place, build the two side walls, making them 4 feet 10 inches high so that a 5-foot length of rigid plastic siding will completely cover the bottom sill. Nail a 1×4 top sill on the side posts.

The most challenging part of this design is cutting the rafter angles. Find the angles for the rafter by using a sheet of 4×4 or larger plywood, cardboard, or heavy paper to mark on. As shown on the diagram at bottom left, draw a pattern for the 2×4 rafters. The exact angle between the roof sections is yours to create, but you will want the lower part of the roof to have a steeper angle than the upper part. Be sure to allow for the thickness of the 2×4 purlin at the rafter joint when you measure and mark your pattern.

Once all the rafter legs have been measured and cut, nail a 2×4 purlin at the top and a 2×4 plate at the bottom of them, as if you were constructing a wall on the ground.

Construct the end walls, door frame, and vent frames with 2×4s. Place the framed lower roof sections on top of the wall and attach them to the end frames. Next add the top rafters on each end and the ridge board, nailing them in place. Then add the remaining top rafters.

A door can be purchased, or built to fit from 1×4s. Add a vent to one side of the door and a fan in the rear end wall.

This barn-style greenhouse can be covered with rigid acrylic panels, double-wall polycarbonate, or two layers of plastic film.

DEFINING TERMS

PURLIN: A rigid support that runs the length of the greenhouse ridge next to it on both sides. Purlins work to support the covering and provide a nailing surface for roof vents. In wooden frame structures, they are usually made from 2×6s, although this plan uses 1×4s.

The solid sidewalls shown here add stability to the barn-style design. Change to rigid plastic or fiberglass if you need more light inside the greenhouse.

MATERIALS LIST

LUMBER: Studs, rafters, sill, braces: 28 2×4s, 8 ft. Ridge board, sill, plates, purlins: 11 2×4s, 10 ft.; 4 2×4s, 8 ft. (Door: see page 32)
COVERING: Rigid acrylic or double-wall polycarbonate panels, or plastic film (to cover approx. 350 sq. ft.)
SUPPLIES: Galvanized nails and wood screws, anchor bolts or rebar, caulk, string, stakes, weather stripping, paint, hinges and door hardware, ridge cap or flashing
TOOLS: Hammer, saw, drill and bits, carpenter's square, level, chalk line, plumb bob, measuring tape

SLANT-SIDED BARN-STYLE GREENHOUSE

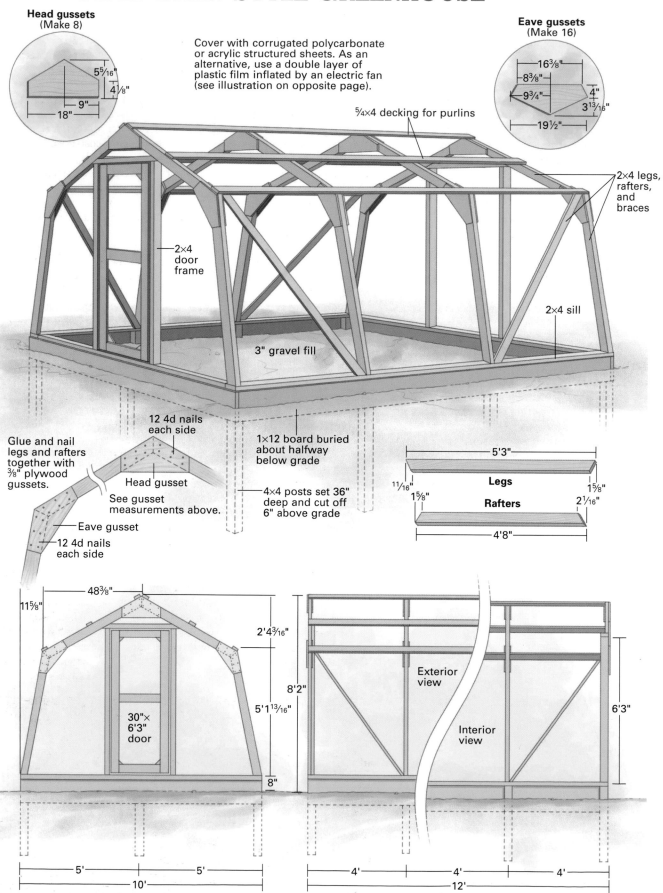

Head gussets
(Make 8)

5⁵/₁₆"
4¹/₈"
9"
18"

Cover with corrugated polycarbonate or acrylic structured sheets. As an alternative, use a double layer of plastic film inflated by an electric fan (see illustration on opposite page).

Eave gussets
(Make 16)

16³/₈"
8³/₈"
9³/₄"
4"
3¹³/₁₆"
19¹/₂"

⁵/₄×4 decking for purlins

2×4 legs, rafters, and braces

2×4 door frame

2×4 sill

3" gravel fill

Glue and nail legs and rafters together with ³/₈" plywood gussets.

12 4d nails each side

Head gusset

See gusset measurements above.

Eave gusset

12 4d nails each side

1×12 board buried about halfway below grade

4×4 posts set 36" deep and cut off 6" above grade

5'3"

11/16"   1⁵/₈"

Legs

1⁵/₈"

Rafters

2¹/₁₆"

4'8"

48³/₈"

11⁵/₈"

2'4³/₁₆"

8'2"

5'1¹³/₁₆"

8"

30"× 6'3" door

Exterior view

Interior view

6'3"

5'   5'

10'

4'   4'   4'

12'

Developed by Professor William Roberts at Rutgers University, this freestanding barn-style greenhouse uses plywood gussets to enhance the structural strength of its slanted sides. It works well where heavy snowfall, windy conditions, or frequent thunderstorms demand a sturdy frame that sheds rain and snow. The gambrel roof is erected in sections and lends itself to plastic film or rigid panel coverings.

To make the head and eave gussets that give this greenhouse its strength, cut one of each as shown in the diagram on the opposite page and use it as a template for all the others. Measure carefully and draw one head gusset and one eave gusset on the plywood, then cut it. A power saw will speed the process of cutting 8 head and 16 eave gussets. Use ⅜-inch exterior plywood to make the gussets. The 2×4 leg and rafter boards likewise require precision cuts, as shown in the detail on the opposite page. After all the pieces are cut, glue and nail or screw the legs and rafters together with the gussets.

For a 10×12-foot greenhouse, the foundation is constructed by sinking ten 4×4s 3 feet into the ground (or 6 inches below the frost line) with enough of the post exposed (approximately 9 inches) to nail the 1×12 frame to it. Dig a 3-inch-deep trench around the perimeter along the 4×4s to sink the 1×12 baseboards slightly below ground level. Trim the top of the 4×4 posts to 6 inches above grade and nail on a 2×4 sill. (For a more permanent foundation, use a poured or concrete-block wall with a sill, then nail the frame onto the sill.)

To frame this greenhouse, first raise the end frames into place; add the end legs and rafters and brace them securely to the sill. Put the two 1×4 purlins on the ridge, then put in the two center legs and rafters and nail them to the purlins. Double-check that everything is square before nailing. Add the purlins at the middle and eave of the roof. Finally, nail in the diagonal side braces to add even more strength to the structure.

Rigid plastic works well on this frame. As an alternative, two layers of flexible plastic film can be used for covering. Systems for inflating plastic are available from companies that sell greenhouse accessories. Or you can put together the simple system illustrated below left. Maintain the thermal barrier layer of air between the plastic layers with a small squirrel-cage blower (30 to 50 cfm with cutoff pressure at less than 0.5-inch water static pressure). Install an adjustable cover over the intake of the blower to control airflow and prevent the plastic from overinflating. Install the fan at one end near the ridgeline by mounting it to a plywood panel suspended from the end rafter. Cut a hole in the plywood for the fan to draw in air. Use flexible plastic tubing and a plastic pot with a hole cut in the bottom as a duct and fitting to direct the air between the two layers of plastic film. The blower will use about 1.4 kW per day.

MATERIALS LIST

LUMBER:
Baseboards: 2 1×12s, 12 ft.; 2 1×12s, 10 ft. (use pressure-treated wood)
Studs, rafters, sill, braces: 24 2×4s, 8 ft.; 2 2×4s, 10 ft.; 2 2×4s, 12 ft.
Purlins: 6 1×4s, 12 ft.
Foundation posts: 5 4×4s, 8 ft. (cut in two for 10 posts; use pressure-treated wood)
Gussets: 2 4×8 sheets ⅜-inch exterior plywood
(Door: see page 32)
COVERING: Rigid plastic panels (to cover approx. 400 sq. ft.)
SUPPLIES: Galvanized nails and wood screws, anchor bolts, caulk, string, stakes, weather stripping, staples, wood glue, paint, hinges and door hardware
TOOLS: Hammer, saw, drill and bits, carpenter's square, level, chalk line, plumb bob, posthole digger, measuring tape

The wide gambrel roof makes room for sunny benches below and fans and lights above. The design lends itself to a single walkway with benches along each side.

DOUBLE-LAYER PLASTIC FILM ASSEMBLY

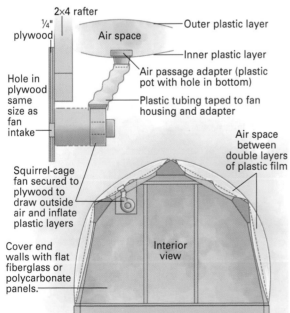

2×4 rafter
¼" plywood
Air space
Outer plastic layer
Inner plastic layer
Air passage adapter (plastic pot with hole in bottom)
Hole in plywood same size as fan intake
Plastic tubing taped to fan housing and adapter
Air space between double layers of plastic film
Squirrel-cage fan secured to plywood to draw outside air and inflate plastic layers
Cover end walls with flat fiberglass or polycarbonate panels.
Interior view

Attach 2 layers of plastic film, one on the outside of the frame and one on the inside. Or use 2×2 spacers between the 2 layers, and lath on top of the outer one.

ATTACHED LEAN-TO GREENHOUSE

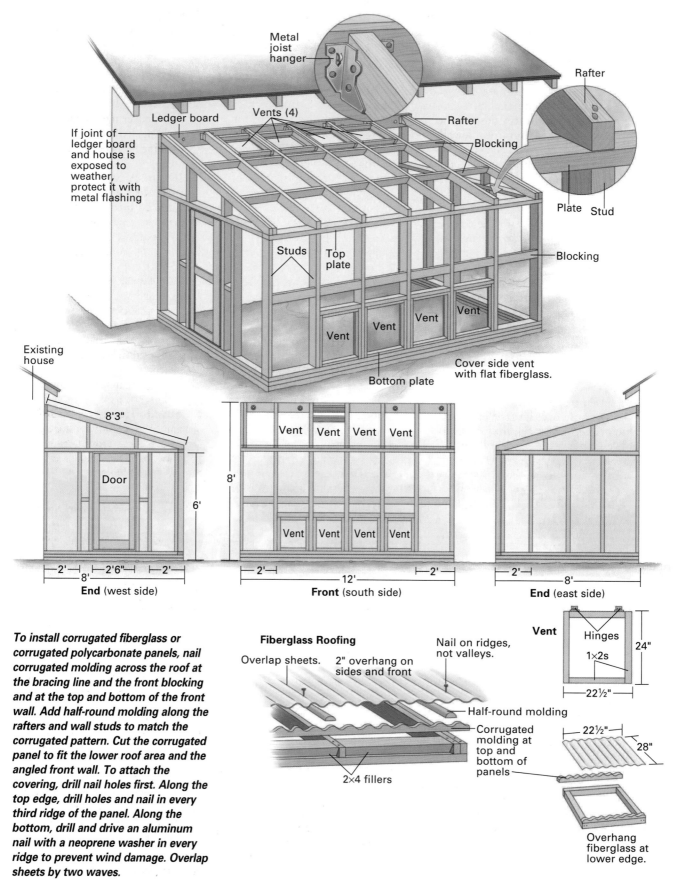

Metal joist hanger

Ledger board

Vents (4)

Rafter

Blocking

Rafter

If joint of ledger board and house is exposed to weather, protect it with metal flashing

Plate   Stud

Studs

Top plate

Blocking

Vent

Vent

Vent

Vent

Bottom plate

Cover side vent with flat fiberglass.

Existing house

8'3"

Door

6'

8'

2'   2'6"   2'

8'

End (west side)

Vent   Vent   Vent   Vent

Vent   Vent   Vent   Vent

2'   12'   2'

Front (south side)

2'   8'

End (east side)

To install corrugated fiberglass or corrugated polycarbonate panels, nail corrugated molding across the roof at the bracing line and the front blocking and at the top and bottom of the front wall. Add half-round molding along the rafters and wall studs to match the corrugated pattern. Cut the corrugated panel to fit the lower roof area and the angled front wall. To attach the covering, drill nail holes first. Along the top edge, drill holes and nail in every third ridge of the panel. Along the bottom, drill and drive an aluminum nail with a neoprene washer in every ridge to prevent wind damage. Overlap sheets by two waves.

Fiberglass Roofing

Overlap sheets.

2" overhang on sides and front

Nail on ridges, not valleys.

Half-round molding

Corrugated molding at top and bottom of panels

2×4 fillers

Vent   Hinges

24"

1×2s

22½"

22½"

28"

Overhang fiberglass at lower edge.

For many gardeners, the most practical of all greenhouses is one that becomes a part of their own home. An attached greenhouse is not only convenient, it is strong and easy to construct because one wall is actually a house wall. Because it is attached to your dwelling, be sure to check local building codes before beginning construction.

This 8×12-foot lean-to is framed with 2×4 redwood or pressure-treated wood and covered with rigid plastic panels. In this design, the roof panels are corrugated and the sidewalls and end walls are not, but you could use flat panels on both. The greenhouse can be built around a door or a window that will connect the greenhouse to the home. Or the greenhouse can attach to a solid house wall, with a door in the end wall for access. The design uses four vents in the outside wall and four in the roof for cooling and air exchange.

Lay out the site, mark the perimeter, and square it. The lightweight frame rests on a simple foundation: Precast concrete piers, spaced 4 feet apart, are sunk in a footing trench with concrete blocks lined between the piers so 2 inches of foundation rises above ground (see page 17). Install a double 2×4 sill by drilling through the sill and bolting it into the foundation.

Most attached greenhouses use a south- or west-facing house wall located under an overhanging eave. First mark the position of the greenhouse along the solid wall. In this plan, headroom is maximized so that the bottom of the ledger board that attaches the greenhouse roof to the house is 8 feet high when used with a 6-foot-high front wall. Next attach the ledger board with lag screws driven into every other stud along the house wall. Use a magnetic stud finder to locate the studs and avoid drilling extra holes.

The lean-to greenhouse can have a basic vertical wall and sloped roof as shown in the diagram opposite, built according to the description on pages 20 and 21. Or you can angle it as shown for the attached greenhouse on page 48. Build the front wall, adapting its vent opening to the desired dimensions for the louvered shutter, an automatic thermal vent, or a simple propped panel.

The end walls are assembled the same way. Allowing for the 3½-inch width of the end studs on the front wall, the plates on the 8-foot end walls are 7 feet 8½ inches long. The studs are 5 feet 9 inches long, spaced 2 feet on center. One wall must accommodate a door. Frame an opening 2 feet 6 inches wide plus ¼ inch for clearance. Use cross braces on each side of the door at knob level to stabilize the door frame.

With the front and end walls in place, frame the roof as described on page 21. To determine the rafter angle, start by placing an uncut 2×4 rafter over the ledger board and the front wall. Mark how the rafter must be cut to fit in the metal joist hanger and angle down to the front wall. Cut it, recheck it, then use it as a pattern for the rest of the rafters. Double the end rafters to simplify nailing in the vertical braces. Frame an opening in the roof to the desired dimensions for an exhaust fan.

Cover the lean-to, beginning with the sides. Each 6-foot-tall sheet of rigid plastic will extend from the top plate past the sill to cover the foundation. You can attach the plastic with nails and lath, or use aluminum extrusions. Remember to drill holes first before nailing into plastic. Butt—do not overlap—the sheets at studs; then nail, seal the joints with caulk, and cover them with lath strips primed and painted white. If you use flat roof panels, install them in the same manner. To ensure a waterproof joint between the ledger board and the house, tuck galvanized metal flashing under the siding and over the ledger and the roof.

See the plan on the facing page for details on installing corrugated fiberglass or corrugated polycarbonate roofing.

Any flooring you prefer can be used in an attached greenhouse, but fine sand or tiny gravel may be tracked into your home. If the flooring is made up of small particles, nail a 1×2 lip inside the greenhouse to contain it in the doorway, and lay down a doormat to wipe your feet as you enter the house.

MATERIALS LIST

LUMBER:
Studs, rafters, sill, plates, braces, blocking: 44 2×4s, 8 ft.; 3 2×4s, 12 ft.; 9 2×4s, 10 ft.
Ledger board: 1 2×6, 12 ft.
Vents: 8 1×2s, 8 ft.
Roof, covering: corrugated molding, half-round molding, redwood or cedar lath
(Door: see page 32)
FOUNDATION: 6 concrete piers, 17 blocks, and concrete ready mix
COVERING: Rigid plastic panels (to cover approx. 280 sq. ft.)
SUPPLIES: Galvanized nails and wood screws, lag screws, 7 angled joist hangers, screws with neoprene washers, anchor bolts, caulk, weather stripping, wood glue, paint, hinges, aluminum flashing, stakes, string
TOOLS: Hammer, saw, drill and bits, carpenter's square, level, mortar trowel, plumb bob, chalk line, measuring tape, stud finder

Rigid acrylic or polycarbonate panels are good covering materials for this attached lean-to greenhouse.

ATTACHED ANGLED-WALL GREENHOUSE

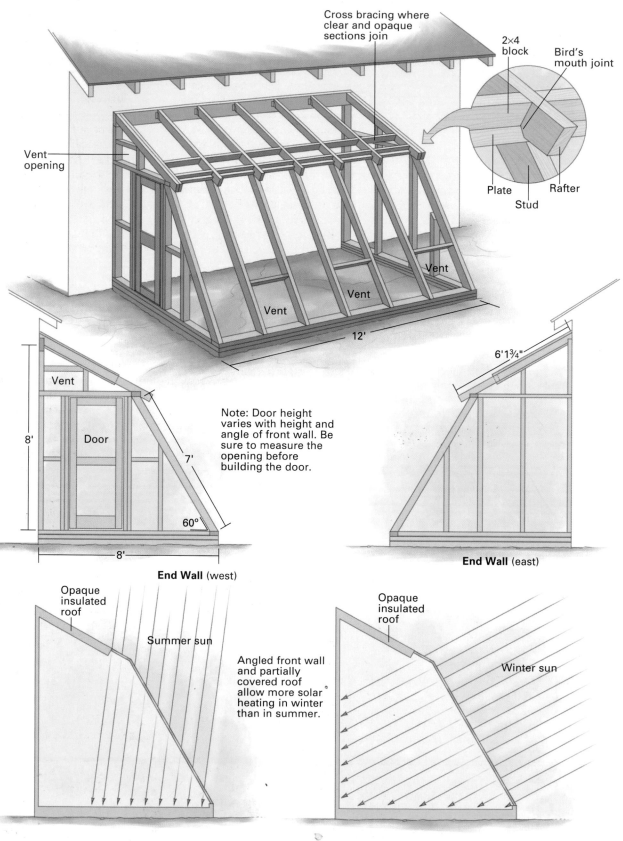

Cross bracing where clear and opaque sections join

2×4 block

Bird's mouth joint

Plate

Stud

Rafter

Vent opening

Vent

Vent

Vent

12'

6'1¾"

Vent

8'

Door

7'

60°

8'

Note: Door height varies with height and angle of front wall. Be sure to measure the opening before building the door.

End Wall (west)

End Wall (east)

Opaque insulated roof

Summer sun

Angled front wall and partially covered roof allow more solar heating in winter than in summer.

Opaque insulated roof

Winter sun

Originally designed by New Mexico builder and solar greenhouse innovator Bill Yanda, the 8×12-foot angled-wall structure shown here is effective in areas with cold but sunny winters and hot summers. It shares qualities with the traditional lean-to and the attached designs. It differs in that the wall is angled to face the low winter sun, and the upper portion of the roof is covered and insulated to give respite from the high summer sun.

This attached greenhouse uses a concrete foundation. Once the sill is in place, determine the optimum angle for your location (see box at right) and cut the wall studs. The 12-foot front wall will host seven studs and seven rafters on 2-foot centers. Remember that the angle of the actual cut is always the difference between the vertical of 90 degrees and the desired angle; that is, for a 60-degree angle, use a protractor to make a 30-degree angle on the bottom of the stud. Make the cut, then cut the top of the stud parallel to the bottom so you can nail on the top plate to lie flat. After you nail the wall together, set it in place and brace it at both ends at the proper angle.

Now put the end walls in place and join their top plate to the front wall's top plate. From this junction, run a stud down to the bottom plate. On the door end, use two studs

nailed together to support the hinge side. Measure the door opening to match the door you will install, plus ¼ inch for clearance, and put up the stud for the other side of the door frame. Add cross braces at doorknob level.

The rafters go up next. Put up a 2×6 ledger board, 12 feet long, and support each rafter with a metal joist support. Seal the connection with aluminum flashing. Where the other end of the rafter attaches to the top plate, cut bird's mouth joints as shown. With the rafters in place, snap a chalk line on the roof two-thirds of the way down from the ledger board or eave to mark where the insulated section stops. Nail 2×4 blocking straight across on this line.

On the front wall between rafters, nail 2×4s so they are flush with the top of the rafters. If a corrugated roof will be used, cover all crosspieces on the roof with strips of corrugated foam or rubber molding.

The upper roof is covered with solid panels of ½-inch exterior-grade plywood, painted or shingled. Add insulation between the rafters and cover with ¼-inch plywood. Corrugated steel could be used for the roof. It is difficult to vent but meshes with the corrugated fiberglass on the walls. Install flashing over the joint between the greenhouse roof and the house wall.

The sidewalls and front wall coverings go on last and are installed in similar fashion. Smooth, rigid acrylic panels could be used instead of corrugated fiberglass.

DEFINING TERMS

OPTIMUM ANGLE: The common angle for solar collection through the greenhouse wall is generally 60 degrees, but another slope may be better for your location. To calculate the optimum angle, add 20 degrees to your geographic latitude. This is the angle between the 7-foot wall stud and the bottom plate (see diagram opposite).

The plantings outside this solar greenhouse shade the inside at summer's peak, and the planting box itself adds needed insulation in winter.

MATERIALS LIST

LUMBER:
Studs, rafters, sill, plates, door frame, braces: 32 2×4s, 8 ft.; 3 2×4s, 12 ft.
Ledger board: 1 2×6, 12 ft.
Roofing: 2 4×8 sheets ½-inch exterior plywood; 2 4×8 sheets ¼-inch exterior plywood
(Door: see page 32)
FOUNDATION: Approx. 20 concrete blocks and concrete ready mix
COVERING: Rigid plastic panels or corrugated fiberglass (to cover approx. 190 sq. ft.); corrugated metal (to cover approx. 48 sq. ft.)
SUPPLIES: Galvanized nails and wood screws, 7 angled joist hangers and lag screws, anchor bolts, caulk, weather stripping, wood glue, paint, hinges, aluminum flashing, stakes, string
TOOLS: Hammer, saw, drill and bits, carpenter's square, level, clamps, chalk line, mortar trowel, measuring tape

ATTACHED SOLAR GREENHOUSE

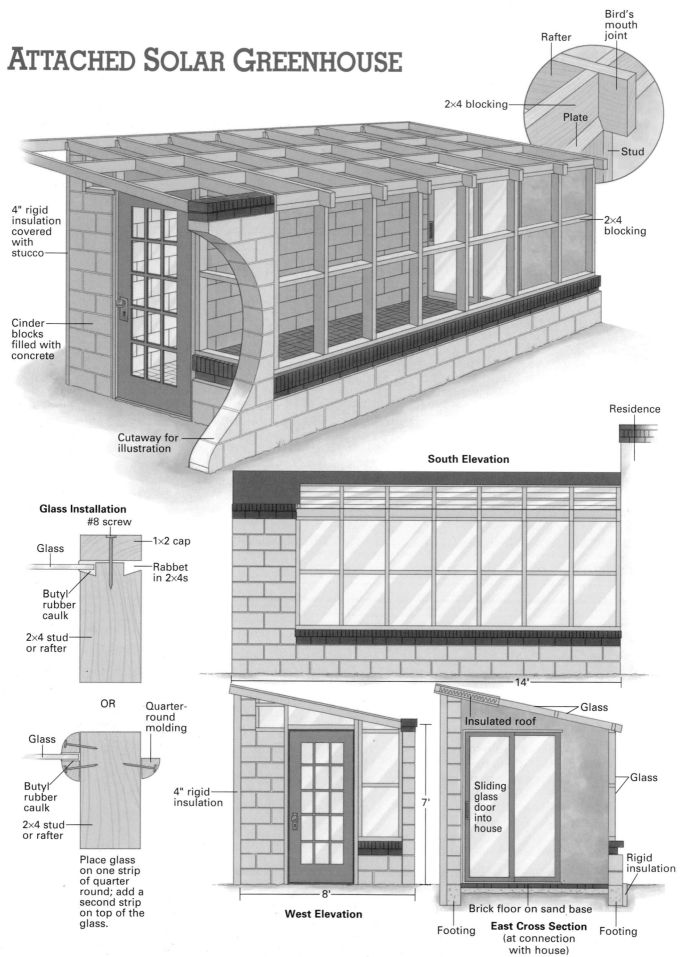

Rafter

Bird's mouth joint

2×4 blocking

Plate

Stud

4" rigid insulation covered with stucco

2×4 blocking

Cinder blocks filled with concrete

Residence

Cutaway for illustration

South Elevation

Glass Installation

#8 screw

1×2 cap

Glass

Rabbet in 2×4s

Butyl rubber caulk

2×4 stud or rafter

OR

Quarter-round molding

Glass

Butyl rubber caulk

2×4 stud or rafter

Place glass on one strip of quarter round; add a second strip on top of the glass.

14'

Glass

Insulated roof

4" rigid insulation

Sliding glass door into house

Glass

7'

Rigid insulation

8'

West Elevation

Footing

Brick floor on sand base

East Cross Section (at connection with house)

Footing

Designed and built by New Mexico landscape architect John Mosely for his own Santa Fe home, this solar greenhouse is attached by a sliding glass door to the house not only for convenience but also to take advantage of greenhouse heat during the winter. In summer, cooler air in the house is vented through the greenhouse to the outside.

The roof of the 8×14-foot glass and redwood structure (pressure-treated wood works, too) is angled for maximum exposure

MATERIALS LIST

LUMBER:
Studs, rafters, sills: 20 2×4s, 8 ft.;
9 2×4s, 10 ft.
Door frame: 3 2×6s, 8 ft.
Fascia board: 1×6, 12 ft.
Roof: 2 4×8 sheets ½-inch exterior plywood
Ceiling: 2 4×8 sheets ¼-inch interior plywood
FOUNDATION: Approx. 220 concrete blocks, depending on depth; concrete ready mix; 2 4×8 sheets 4-inch rigid insulation
COVERING: Double-strength glass (to cover approx. 190 sq. ft.), lath strips (22 8-ft. pieces) and/or quarter-round molding (80 8-ft. pieces)
SUPPLIES: Galvanized nails, wood screws, lag screws, anchor bolts, butyl rubber caulk, weather stripping, wood glue, paint, hinges, aluminum flashing, stakes, string
TOOLS: Measuring tape, hammer, saw, drill and bits, carpenter's square, level, clamps, chalk line, mortar trowel

the footing with rigid insulation braced against the excavated wall. Pour the concrete. When the footing has hardened, build the walls with standard size concrete blocks; top the walls with 2×4 or 2×6 sills.

To install the glass, cut rabbets on each side of each vertical stud, plus the top and bottom plates and the crosspieces, to receive the panes. If you do not have access to a table saw or router for rabbeting, you can install the glass using quarter-round molding or 1×1 redwood strips as stops nailed across studs and rafters.

The next step is to frame the west wall, which holds the exterior door. The door frame goes in first, then the top plate, the door header, and the window and vent frames.

Once the front and side walls are in place, it is time to measure and lay the roof. Rafters should overhang the walls by several inches for drainage. Cut the front (bottom) end of the rafters with a bird's mouth joint to fit the top plate of the front wall. Notch the back (top) of the rafter to fit the top plate of the back wall. Rabbet each rafter and block for the glass as you did the front wall. Nail the rafters in place; then nail in blocking between the rafters at the front wall sill. Nail 1×6 fascia boards to cover the ends of the rafters. Place insulation between the rafters under the covered roof section. Nail ¼-inch plywood on the interior ceiling.

Install the glass in the remaining portion of the roof, sealing each piece on both sides with butyl rubber caulk or glazing compound. Use 1×2 strips to hold the glass in place.

This solar greenhouse is glazed with double-strength glass, an appropriate choice for this design in an arid climate. In rainy climates, a covering of rigid acrylic or polyethylene panels held in place by extruded metal framing would shed rain more efficiently.

to the sun. The upper third of the roof is covered with insulation to provide relief from the overhead summer sun.

The 14-foot-wide north wall, made from concrete block filled with concrete, acts as a heat sink. The outside of this 8-foot-high wall is insulated with 4-inch-thick rigid insulation, which is covered with stucco to protect it from the weather.

Consult local building codes to be sure the greenhouse meets requirements. Mosely extended the block wall to meet local codes. You may not need the added wall to meet your codes, but consider it to create an outdoor work space for potting or storage.

Begin the construction by laying out the site and excavating so the greenhouse floor will be level with that of the house. Position forms of 2×8s for the footing around the inside perimeter and level them. Form the outside of

WORKING WITH KITS

This attached kit comes with your choice of glass or polycarbonate panels.

Curved eaves, automatic vents, and double-wall polycarbonate covering are features of this 12×16-foot kit.

Kit greenhouses have one big advantage for busy people: All the parts arrive at once in boxes delivered to your house. Besides shopping convenience, many kits offer an aluminum frame with channels that make covering the structure simple. You will still have to build a foundation and arrange for utilities to be connected, but most kit greenhouses can be assembled by two people in less than two days.

Building a greenhouse from a kit can guide your equipment choices. Consider dealing with a greenhouse supplier who also offers a line of sturdy accessories. Although prices for general-purpose items at a discount store may be tempting, the equipment suggested for a particular kit is designed to fit without altering or damaging the structure or voiding its warranties.

POPULAR MODELS

Many models are available from greenhouse suppliers, and you should review several before deciding what to buy. Manufacturers offer attached and freestanding greenhouses in a variety of sizes, many expandable to suit your needs. You will find curved and straight eaves and various systems for roof, end, and side vents. Wood frames and several gauges of aluminum and steel frames are offered, and coverings of tempered glass, double- or triple-wall rigid plastic panels, and clear plastic sheets. Some suppliers also offer frames alone that you can cover with plastic film.

EVALUATING KITS

As a general rule, the most expensive kits are for complicated designs and include everything you need, down to the nuts and bolts. The spectrum of kits runs from top-dollar models through simpler designs in complete kits to models that require additional shopping to complete. The more materials you have to provide, such as covers, hardware, and vents, the less the kit will cost. But those less expensive kits may be more complicated to put together. In evaluating kits, you should consider both cost and ease of assembly.

To calculate the true cost of your greenhouse, start with the price of the kit, any applicable taxes, and shipping, which can be expensive. Next add the cost of the foundation and utility connections. Finally, check the kit information to estimate the time it will take to complete the project. If you plan to hire labor to help, add that cost.

Consider carefully your skills and available time. The amount of work involved in assembling a greenhouse may be a deciding factor in choosing a kit. Look over the instructions in the kit and see if they match your skill level.

In many top-end kits, all structural components are predrilled and the panels are cut to fit, if not already preassembled. But the convenience usually comes at a price.

In less expensive but comparable structures, you may find yourself cutting panels, drilling holes, and making minor adjustments before you screw pieces together.

Consult with the manufacturer before purchase if you have questions about assembly, because this information is not always clearly stated in a catalog or brochure.

USING THIS BOOK WITH A KIT GREENHOUSE

Each aspect of building a kit greenhouse corresponds to one in building a similar design from scratch. Read this book or refer to specific sections to become familiar with foundations, utility hookups, coverings, shade options, and management practices.

Your kit greenhouse must meet any building codes that apply, and all utilities must meet local codes for safe operation. It is imperative that you build a square and level foundation before you start construction. Refer to the sections in this book that discuss these important steps in the process.

When your kit arrives, open it, unpack everything onto a tarp so you can see the pieces clearly, and compare the packing list with the contents to be certain it is the greenhouse you ordered. Contact the supplier immediately if any parts are missing.

Once all the parts are accounted for, the foundation is in place, and the weather is cooperative, you are ready to proceed. Study the plans thoroughly again. Building a greenhouse from a kit is like working on a jigsaw puzzle; each piece must be placed in its proper position in the right order. Do not take shortcuts or skip steps.

Following the directions is crucial to building a tight greenhouse that will stand for years. Failure to do so can create hazards and slow construction, and may violate warranties.

Available through mail order or some home centers, a small starter greenhouse kit usually costs less than $1,000.

This model's high-tech glazing and solar design maximize light transmission.

TIPS FOR OWNERS OF KIT GREENHOUSES

Buy a repair kit from the supplier at the same time you purchase the greenhouse. Although most greenhouses will remain in good shape long after their warranties expire, accidents can happen. You'll be ready to patch the covering temporarily, and your plants won't suffer even if the temperature drops to 20 degrees outside.

Although most wooden members of a greenhouse structure are made of rot-resistant or pressure-treated lumber, you may want to give them extra protection with a waterproofing stain, or paint them white to reflect sunlight into the growing space. You can do this either before or after assembly.

If you choose a less expensive structure with low headroom, seriously consider installing it on top of a foundation knee wall. Read page 17 to learn how.

Trees near greenhouses, especially those covered with flexible plastic film, need to be kept properly pruned. Fallen branches can easily puncture and destroy the covering.

BENCHES AND EQUIPMENT

Build benches to your personal specifications: Use any length, but adjust bench width to arm length. Although benches are usually 28 to 32 inches off the floor for maximum air circulation and growing below, they can easily be set lower and narrowed for wheelchair access.

Equipment accounts for a significant portion of greenhouse expense. Carefully choosing the right equipment before you plan and build your greenhouse allows you to make the most of your money as well as end up with a greenhouse that will provide you with years of growing success. This chapter outlines the important items you might need or want to furnish the growing space. Benches are the largest structures in the greenhouse, and their layout and design will have a big impact on greenhouse efficiency and usability. They are joined by essential tools and necessary supplies, as well as accessories and devices you can set up for rooting and seeding. In this chapter you will also learn about equipment to provide water and fertilizer efficiently, including automated systems that can save you time and money.

BENCHES

Ideally, greenhouse benches will be both practical and good-looking. They should provide sufficient display area for plants, with growing room and ample sunlight for every pot. They must be constructed to allow maximum airflow through them and among the plants, including 2 inches of space between the back of the bench and the greenhouse wall if benches are topped with wooden slats. They should be clean, have no sharp edges to catch your sleeve, and be sturdy enough to hold pots without sagging. A bench should be nearly as wide as your reach (usually less than 36 inches) with plenty of room for an accessible aisle at least 16 inches wide. A bench that has access from both sides can be as wide as 66 inches.

A variety of metal, plastic, and wooden greenhouse benches are available ready-made from greenhouse supply companies. Or you can save considerable expense and enjoy benches custom-built to your needs by constructing your own. You can build benches with the plans in this chapter or adapt the plans to suit your space and style.

If you do not have room in or near the greenhouse for a dedicated potting area, plan to use a bench or part of one. You can incorporate a sink and potting bench as well as a storage section into the darkest bench space, or the one nearest the utilities.

BENCH LAYOUTS

The bench arrangement serves an obvious purpose, but it also sets a mood and directs traffic in the greenhouse. How benches are laid out is important. A north-south orientation is preferable to ensure an even distribution of light as the sun moves from east to west. Usually the bench layout follows either an aisle or a peninsula plan.

The aisle layout features two rows of benches, generally along each side of the greenhouse to conserve space, with an aisle between. A common arrangement in hobby greenhouses, the aisle layout often features a small sink and potting area on the north side or built into one bench.

The peninsula layout has individual benches perpendicular to the side walls, with very narrow aisles between the benches and a wider aisle down the middle. If the greenhouse is big enough, the peninsula plan is probably more satisfactory, because there is room in the center aisle for tall plants that are brought inside for the winter.

Either bench arrangement can be adapted for your comfort. Before you construct a bench, be sure it will accommodate your needs. A typical height is 28 to 32 inches. If you will garden standing up, stand in the aisle and reach across the bench space. If you cannot reach what will be the bench back without bending in half, consider narrowing the bench width or raising its top until you are comfortable. You may want to put a rooting box on a higher bench, or lower the whole arrangement to accommodate you when seated.

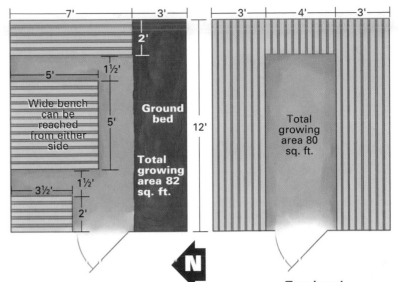

Two bench layouts for a 10×12-foot greenhouse. Left: Peninsula layout with ground bed. Right: Aisle layout. Both layouts yield nearly identical growing space.

CHOOSING MATERIALS

When you choose wood to build the greenhouse bench or top, use pressure-treated products for long life. Some kit benches are made of the same durable cedar or redwood recommended for the structure, but this lumber can be expensive to purchase for a do-it-yourself project.

Slatted bench tops offer the advantages of wood but provide less air circulation and age much faster than wire mesh hardware cloth tops. The bench top can, though, be made of any material that is strong enough to hold pots, drains well, and can be cleaned if soil or mold build up. Recycled lath, disassembled shipping crates, and even plastic bread trays can be used as bench tops, although wooden materials will not last long unless treated.

Use the longest possible wood screws to put the benches together. Anytime you want to screw two pieces of wood together, first drill a pilot hole. A pilot hole enables the screw to bite into the wood on the first try. The cleaner the assembly, the less chance the wood will split.

BENCH STYLES

Style in greenhouse benches depends on the materials used and how you arrange the components. Two basic benches with wood slat tops flanking a gravel path create a warm, welcoming space for all who look inside. A peninsula arrangement topped with wire mesh hardware cloth separated by solid concrete walkways sends a much more formal message.

Let your plant collecting habits dictate bench styles. If you plan to maintain tall and short plants, grow some vegetables, start some seeds, and keep the neighbor's cactus, too, plan for it. Put a basic bench on one side, but use component benches along the opposite wall to add as you need them. Or use plastic shelving in different heights to make room for tall plants, small pots, and hanging baskets.

Although the aisle or peninsula bench layout will work in most greenhouses, the style of the benches can be as individual as your plant collection. Because they are a part of the house, attached greenhouses often incorporate stylish benches. Baker's racks and wrought-iron tables meet basic bench criteria and add a touch of class and coordination with interior furnishings.

The choice of more conventional bench materials affects style in practical and aesthetic ways. Although pipe bench frames, either galvanized or rigid plastic, can be cold to the touch and don't offer the classic warmth of wood, they have one distinct shape advantage over wood. They are rounded, so they shed water and dirt readily. Bolting pipes may not be any more difficult than screwing wood together. Some pipes are an attractive white color or can be painted. They look sleek and modern—and pipe benches should last virtually forever.

Expanded metal benches are long-lasting and sturdy. They are available through professional greenhouse supply companies.

BUILDING BENCHES

Y ou can make a simple, practical greenhouse bench from 2×4 legs, rails, and braces and a top of 1×4 boards. The lumber should be redwood or pressure-treated to extend its life. The top boards should extend about 6 inches on the aisle side of the rails. Benches along the sidewall can be up to 36 inches wide. A bench in the center can be up to 66 inches wide but will need an extra rail in the center to keep the top boards from sagging.

BASIC BENCH

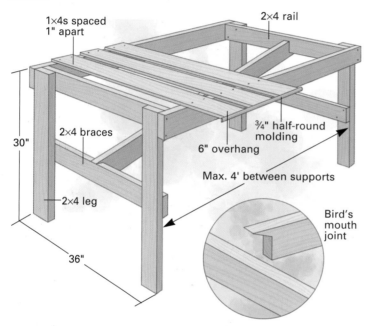

1×4s spaced 1" apart
2×4 rail
30"
2×4 braces
2×4 leg
36"
¾" half-round molding
6" overhang
Max. 4' between supports
Bird's mouth joint

Put the support frames in place in the greenhouse with patio blocks or bricks under the legs. These will keep the bench level. Attach the 2×4 top and bracing. Add any center support frames. Now level the bench assembly by adjusting the supporting blocks.

Top the frame with the 1×4s, leaving about 1 inch between boards. Galvanized ring nails or screws will hold the boards in place. Finish the front exposed edge with a ¾-inch half-round molding.

COMPONENT CONSTRUCTION

A component bench can be built in pieces to create a structure of any length, using the plan shown at left with several modifications.

The leg components are built from 2×4s as shown with two changes. For the top of the leg supports, use two 2×4s, cut to length to provide a 6-inch overhang. Attach them perpendicularly to each side of the legs, so that the legs are sandwiched between them.

To create a storage shelf, attach the lower braces one-third the distance up from the bottom of each leg. Place boards across these once the components are in place.

When the leg components are all complete, nail on 1×8s lengthwise horizontally across the top, spacing them 1 inch apart. Attach top boards to the legs with nails or screws. If the bench frame is too long for single lengths of 1×8s, join the boards on alternate legs.

CONCRETE BLOCK AND GALVANIZED PIPE BENCHES

As an alternative to wood, you can use pipe and concrete blocks to build a strong bench. The simplest method is to stack up concrete blocks three or four high to form the legs for the bench. They can be stacked dry without mortar. Arrange the stacks about 4 feet apart on a square pattern the length of the greenhouse wall. Top them with a 2×4 frame and bench wire as described below.

You can make a pipe-framed bench from 1¼-inch galvanized water pipe or fence tubing. Build the framework first, using fence fittings and couplings to join legs, top rails, and braces. Set the legs of the completed framework in the holes of concrete blocks; level the frame and brace it temporarily. Pour concrete in the holes, checking the level frequently. When the concrete is set, cover the top with a heavy wire mesh and attach it with screws and washers (see photograph page 57).

MATERIALS LIST

LUMBER:
Frame: 6 2×4s, 8 ft.;
Slats: 6 1×4s, 8 ft.
SUPPLIES:
Galvanized nails and wood screws, paint
TOOLS: Hammer, carpenter's square, level, saw, drill and bits, screwdriver, measuring tape

Measure your comfort zone to make the height of the bench convenient. Typical height is 28 to 32 inches. The length of the bench can fit the space that you have available. The legs should be evenly spaced and no more than 4 feet apart. A brace can be installed as shown, or a second rail from 2×4s could be attached about halfway down the leg to provide bracing. Use three or four galvanized deck screws in each joint to give it strength. For added strength use bird's mouth joints as shown.

Construction should be done on a flat surface such as a garage or basement floor, paved driveway, or the floor of the greenhouse. Build the support frames first. Use a framing square to be sure the legs are perpendicular to the brace. Make as many support frames as needed.

BENCH TOPS

A 2×4 frame covered with mesh of 10- or 12½-gauge wire will give many years of service without sagging. The mesh should be either galvanized or coated with vinyl for a smoother surface and longer life. A better choice used by most commercial growers is galvanized, expanded metal made from a sheet of thin steel that has been slit and then expanded to 10 times its original size. A 13-gauge, ¾-inch opening is standard for benches. The diamond-shaped openings give this material better strength and rigidity than the wire mesh.

Rigid plastic bench tops and plastic-coated wire utility shelving are becoming increasingly popular. Greenhouse supply companies sell a variety of such bench tops in standard sizes. To outfit a small greenhouse or to add benches as you need them, check out rigid plastic shelves designed for storage or office use. The best of these feature wide leg pipes and heavy grid tops that can support considerable weight. Coated closet shelving, usually white, reflects light onto plants, and the spacing of its thin yet sturdy wire supports allows ample air circulation to promote healthy plants.

SHELVES, RACKS, AND HANGERS

The space overhead in the greenhouse is valuable for growing plants that like a warmer temperature and more light. By attaching hooks to the roof support bars or attaching shelves or pipes to the greenhouse walls, you can accommodate many additional plants. Most greenhouse suppliers offer brackets for attaching shelves or pipes to the greenhouse walls. Be careful not to overload the roof.

A wooden step bench can be made to fit along a greenhouse wall. The width of the steps should fit the containers that will be used. Besides increasing bench space, step benches show off plants effectively.

BEDS

Growing beds placed on the floor are excellent for tall plants, such as tomatoes, cucumbers, and roses. A bed can be dug into the floor soil, although it may need to have peat moss added for good drainage. Or you could build a plastic-lined wooden frame to set on the floor, and fill it with growing mix. Hydroponic setups, including a box of pea stone, several bags of growing mix, or a nutrient-film technique (NFT) plastic channel will also work well on the floor (see pages 82 and 83). The width of the growing area should be limited to a convenient reach. Support from overhead may be needed to tie up taller plants.

Above: Don't leave sharp edges exposed on wire bench tops. Use close-meshed, sturdy steel strong enough to support heavy containers.
Left: A simple raised bed capitalizes on floor space.
Below: Racks, shelves, hangers, and wide, lipped benches maximize the growing area.

POTTING AREAS, SEED STARTERS, MIST SYSTEMS

A designated potting area establishes a useful, organized space that stays clean and dry to promote good sanitation. A raised edge keeps soil contained for mixing and potting.

MATERIALS LIST

LUMBER: 2 1×4s or 1×6s, 8 ft. (3'×4' bench)
SUPPLIES: Galvanized nails and wood screws, paint, plastic film
TOOLS: Hammer, saw, drill and bits, carpenter's square, level, staple gun, measuring tape

BENCHES AND ROOTING BOXES

Potting areas often tell much about a gardener. Some are simple, temporary tables set up as needed with a wheelbarrow full of soil mix at the ready. More permanent arrangements include shelves above and storage below, supplies and tools neatly stored. When you see a radio and portable telephone in the potting area, you know the place is as much a retreat as anything else.

Many gardeners prefer to locate their potting area outside the greenhouse, covered with lath or built like a utility room attached to the greenhouse. But to use the potting area year-round in snowy regions, put it inside the greenhouse on a bench in the northwest corner. You can use a slatted bench top with a simple lip if a growing area below can take the soil that falls through. But if you want clean storage underneath or have wire bench tops, build the box shown below instead of attaching the wooden lip to the bench itself.

This simple box easily adapts to make a rooting chamber using 1×6s instead of 1×4s. You can enclose it with the same framed plastic cover shown on page 59 for a seed starter, but instead of putting the cover over flats, measure it to stand on top of the chamber frame to allow more headroom for growing cuttings.

SEED STARTERS

A simple, effective, and inexpensive seed-starting chamber consists of a wooden frame, plastic film, seed flats, bottom irrigation reservoirs, wire mesh, and a heating cable. Nail 1×4s together to form a frame just larger than two seed flats; cover it with clear polyethylene film, overlap all sides, and staple it to the frame. Place a piece of plywood or 6-mil plastic film on a bench and spread a 1-inch layer of fine gravel or sand on top. Next lay the heating cable in a serpentine pattern with no wires crossing. Cover the cable with another inch of sand, then lay wire mesh hardware cloth over the sand. On the wire mesh, place one or two shallow plastic trays that fit beneath your seed flats to supply constant water and occasional fertilizer. To regulate soil temperature in the seedling soil mix, insert a remote sensor connected to a thermostat. Note: To prevent overheating the seedlings, seed starters should be placed on the bench out of direct sunlight.

BOTTOM HEAT

A thermostatically controlled heating cable will be your best friend when it comes to rooting plants and sprouting seeds. The difference in your success rate with either project will be measurable. Heating cables come in various lengths; buy enough to lay out a serpentine pattern that is uniformly spaced and does not cross itself.

Heating cables should be controlled by a thermostat; be sure to turn off the cable

POTTING BENCH

1×4 frame for box

Basic bench *(see page 56)* with additional box sitting or attached on top

Box with solid bottom

PORTABLE POTTING TRAY

in summer to avoid overheating roots. Take extra safety precautions when using a heating cable in wet areas, and always connect it to a GFCI outlet (see page 19). Never allow cables to touch plastic trays.

MULTIPLYING UNDER MIST

A mist system will speed the rooting of soft or woody cuttings and provide quality plants. The object of misting is to maintain a film of moisture on the leaves until roots form. It reduces transpiration and allows the cuttings to be propagated in full sunlight without wilting or becoming excessively dehydrated. Apply only enough mist to keep foliage wet so that plants don't wilt. Excessive water will flood the bench or containers and keep the growing medium too cool.

Most cuttings root best at a daytime temperature of 70 to 80 degrees F and a night-time temperature about 10 degrees cooler. An electric propagation mat or heating cable with thermostatic control can be used to provide bottom heat.

An enclosed mist chamber can be added to a bench, or you can adapt the rooting box plan. If you are building the chamber on the bench, add a piece of treated plywood to the bottom of the bench so that the soil will not fall through. Build a frame around the plywood out of treated 1×6s. Place a layer of gravel on the bottom, then add 4 inches of perlite. The cuttings are inserted in the perlite for rooting. You can also use this system for rooting cuttings in flats or pots. Just eliminate the 4 inches of perlite, and place the containers directly on the gravel.

There are two systems for supporting nozzles above cuttings. One uses a supply pipe fastened to the bench bottom that supports risers with mist nozzles mounted at the top. The risers should be 12 to 18 inches above the cuttings. Nozzles are usually spaced 3 feet apart for a uniform spray pattern.

In the second system, the pipe, with nozzles spaced every 3 feet, is supported about 18 inches above the bench on a cable or furring strip. The cable can be attached to the end walls of the greenhouse. The furring strip is supported by an A-frame made from 2×2s or ½-inch conduit.

Water for the mist line can come from a hose faucet. It should be connected to a 140-mesh filter, a 30-psi pressure regulator, and a 24-volt solenoid valve. The valve that turns on the mist is connected to a single-zone controller. The controller has settings for watering time, cycle time, and duration of watering cycles.

An alternative device, the Mist-A-Matic control, simulates a leaf in the propagating bed. It consists of a piece of stainless steel screen attached to an electric switch that is placed in the bed area. When the screen is dry, it activates the switch and the solenoid valve in the water supply line. When it gets wet, it gets heavier and turns off the valve. On sunny days when evaporation is greater, the system cycles on more frequently.

Usually the mist chamber is enclosed with vertical plastic film sheets to prevent mist from drifting. The plastic should extend from the bench top to above the nozzles. Attach the plastic with clothespins to wires suspended above the bench.

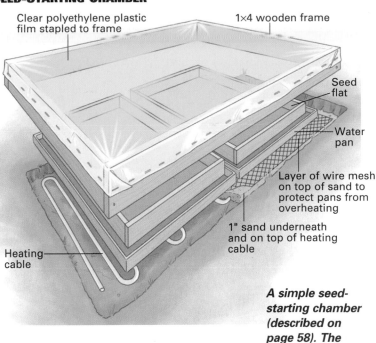

SEED-STARTING CHAMBER

Clear polyethylene plastic film stapled to frame

1×4 wooden frame

Seed flat

Water pan

Layer of wire mesh on top of sand to protect pans from overheating

1" sand underneath and on top of heating cable

Heating cable

A simple seed-starting chamber (described on page 58). The layer of wire mesh is essential to prevent pans from overheating.

MIST SYSTEM PLUMBING

Water supply

Globe valve

Pressure regulator

Pressure gauge

Hose faucet

Pipe union

24-volt electric solenoid valve

Water to mist or irrigation system

MIST PROPAGATION BENCH

½" riser with mister nozzle 18" above soil level

2" rooting mix or wooden flats on top of sand

2" sand

Bench bottom

Water pipe to solenoid valve and timer

Heating cable should be uniformly spaced and never cross itself.

1" gravel

TOOLS AND SUPPLIES

Greenhouse hand tools do what your hands alone can't do, and they speed your work. Many are the same as the tools you use in the outdoor garden, but for the sake of sanitation, gather a separate set and keep them in the greenhouse.

The quality of traditional hand tools improves with each innovation. Look for forged one-piece construction for durability, and ergonomic designs, including padded handles, for comfort.

Start with two kinds of gloves. Select one pair of any fabric that lets your fingers work unfettered but protected. Use heavy-duty latex rubber gloves for handling caustics such as bleach and pesticide sprays. Use pruning shears to cut plants, but keep scissors on hand for other tasks. Use hand trowels to dig soil mixes, and keep a simple scoop inside each bag of ingredients to keep them clean. You will need a shovel and a stiff-tined rake—handy in any greenhouse and essential if you use large pots or floor beds. Both are available in a variety of sizes.

Hand-watering tools include both cans and hoses fitted with special spouts or water-breaking nozzles. A 2-quart, narrow-spouted watering can and a 3-gallon model with a rose (a round-patterned breaking nozzle) can handle most tasks. The water hose should reach the entire length of the greenhouse plus a few feet. Three kinds of nozzles will meet nearly all watering needs: a pressure nozzle to clean walkways and walls, a round or fan pattern nozzle for primary watering, and a mist nozzle to add moisture to the air between irrigations.

Collect, install, and use a variety of measuring devices to stay in tune with greenhouse conditions. Put thermometers inside and out, on the bench and attached to the uprights. Distribute rain gauges along the bench to measure overhead sprinkler output.

TOOL AND SUPPLY CHECKLIST

TOOLS
■ Trowels
■ Scoop for each container
■ Pruning shears
■ Scissors
■ Stiff-tined garden rake
■ Gloves
■ Hose
■ Nozzles
■ Plant labels, waterproof marking pen

SUPPLIES
■ **POTS:** Plastic, clay, and peat pots; flats and trays
■ **SOIL MIX COMPONENTS:** Peat, sand, perlite, and a selection of commercial potting soil mixes
■ **CHEMICALS:** Soluble, granular, and timed-release fertilizers; rooting hormones; lime
■ **PEST CONTROL:** Traps, monitors, pesticides

ESSENTIAL SUPPLIES

The growing supplies you keep on hand will depend on your plants and work habits. It's likely you will accumulate more for specific projects, but the suggested supply list at left will more than get you started. Plant containers should include plastic flats and three kinds of pots: plastic, clay, and peat fiber. Peat pots and compressed peat pellets are for seedlings that are difficult to transplant. Clay pots are best for large plants, cacti, and succulents, particularly with overhead watering systems. Plastic pots get the most use in bench growing. Keep several sizes on hand: 4-inch and 6-inch pots, 10-inch, shallow but wide bowls, and hanging baskets. If you reuse pots and flats, clean them thoroughly with a solution of 1 part bleach to 9 parts water.

Store each kind of growing media that you keep on hand in its own labeled, covered container. The same goes for fertilizers; label and store each separately. It is important to keep both solubles and granular fertilizers in watertight containers; humidity destroys their effectiveness. If you store soil amendments or fertilizers in bags at ground level, elevate the holding area with a slatted floor, perhaps made from a wooden shipping pallet.

Other useful supplies include garden or horticultural lime (not hydrated) in powder or pellet form, and rooting hormone. Clean and sanitize tools with household bleach, kept with other chemicals in a locked cabinet. Good greenhouse practice is to purchase pesticides only as needed and in the smallest amounts possible to limit the need for storage. To monitor pests, use two kinds of insect traps: yellow and blue sticky bars for flying insects and a baited box for crawling pests.

BASIC EQUIPMENT AND HANDY EXTRAS

You'll find the following equipment helpful to establish and control growing conditions. Use a hygrometer to be sure you are maintaining 60 percent relative humidity, higher for tropical plants. Locate one thermometer at each end of the greenhouse at a different height, protected from direct sun and shielded in a box. To ensure that the heating system is working properly, you should check the thermometer frequently, even at night. For easier temperature monitoring, use a maximum-minimum thermometer to display the temperature range on a daily basis. If a growing bed on the greenhouse floor isn't productive, you may want to monitor its temperature with a soil thermometer. A soil thermometer is also handy to monitor the output of heating cables. A rain gauge on the bench under an overhead irrigation system alerts you to its flow and timing sequences.

A minimum of two sprayers is useful in the greenhouse: a hand spritzer to clean leaves and increase humidity, and a 1- or 2-gallon pump-up pressure sprayer for applying chemicals. A pump-up pressure sprayer, with its restricted flow, works better than a watering can to water and fertilize seedlings, but if you use it for this purpose, be sure it is dedicated solely to watering and never used for chemicals. Keep a set of plastic (not metal) measuring cups and spoons in the greenhouse; wash with soap and water after every use. Never use greenhouse equipment to mix or spray chemicals for weed control.

Other essential equipment includes storage containers: a trash can, a compost bucket, and containers of various sizes ranging from 30-gallon trash cans for soil mixes to screw-top jars for powdered rooting hormone. Clean and dry containers thoroughly before using them for storage, especially if they are recycled. Keep a broom and dustpan nearby. If you don't have a potting area, use a wheelbarrow for mixing soil, and lay a scrap piece of plywood on top for an instant potting bench.

Complete your list of essentials with plastic labels, a permanent marker, mesh onion bags, and a roll of jute string. You will certainly want a calendar and a greenhouse journal. You may want a radio and sunscreen, too. More devices and monitoring gizmos will appeal to you for one project or another. A watering wand extends your arm to reach hanging plants or the back of the bench. Trellises lift leaves toward the sun and save space below for more pots. Where water quality is a concern, use a test kit to keep abreast of changing conditions.

STORAGE

Think up, down, and overhead when planning for greenhouse storage. Every shady nook has potential to hold supplies, tools, and equipment, especially if you have a potting area in or near the structure. Start by installing a shelf over the bench to hold pots, small bags, gloves, and tools. Put brackets on the wall to hold the shelf, or stand a small unit along the back of the bench.

You can create a storage area under the bench by running 1×4s across the braces to form a slatted shelf. If you have small children or intend to store chemicals, enclose the area with exterior plywood, and add locking doors.

If the shape of your greenhouse permits, use 1×12s to build overhead shelving boxes to stand above the bench along the north wall. Vary the size of the boxes, but make them deep: perhaps 6, 12, and 18 inches square and 2 feet deep. Mount the boxes on the wall or stack them and bolt or screw them together.

A tool rack to hang shears, trowels, rakes, brooms, and other handled tools makes a convenient addition to the potting area. Use perforated board cut to fit the available area, perhaps the space between two or three pieces of the greenhouse frame. You can locate the tool rack along the wall next to the bench, or overhead attached to the joists for seldom-used tools. The space between the frames accommodates the metal hangers, or you can use furring strips to raise the board away from a solid wall.

Arrange a storage area for easy reach and return, then use it to keep frequently used tools and equipment handy. Lock up chemicals and sharp-bladed tools for safety.

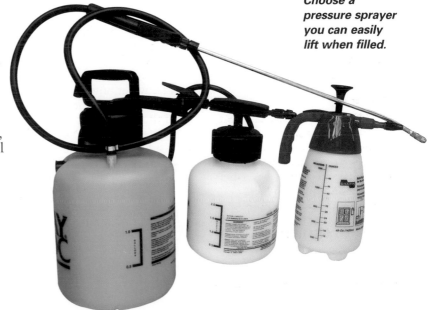

Choose a pressure sprayer you can easily lift when filled.

WATERING SYSTEMS

Water breakers and nozzles with varied patterns can irrigate efficiently without splashing soil out of containers or causing unnecessary puddling. Use drip irrigation to conserve water and aluminum wands to extend your reach neatly.

The most common method for irrigating greenhouse plants is hand-watering with a garden hose or watering can. Overhead sprinklers and misters, drip irrigation, and capillary matting can also be used, although they are most practical when you have a large greenhouse or are growing plants of similar needs in containers of the same size. Whichever system you use, group plants on the bench according to their moisture needs, and time your watering regime so that leaves dry out by nightfall.

Most greenhouse plants are watered by hand, even though a large collection takes considerable time to irrigate. The process gives you the chance to observe each plant individually to determine its needs. Unlike other methods, hand-watering lets you tend some plants and skip others. Use nozzles— a water breaker or fan spray head on the hose or a rose attachment on the watering can. They slow the flow of water and direct it into gentle, rainlike patterns that irrigate without washing soil out of the pots. Keep the nozzles clean and off the floor, where they could pick up bacteria and other disease-causing organisms.

With careful management, overhead sprinklers can work well in the greenhouse. Look for low-volume sprinkler systems to save on water and give you more control over the spray pattern. You can attach the water supply to the bench and elevate the sprinklers appropriately, usually 18 to 24 inches above the plants. Many greenhouse gardeners water by hand most of the time, then use a sprinkler system for a twice-weekly dousing of the entire bench at once. Sprinklers, like mist systems, raise the humidity, which can be essential for midday relief in dry climates or at the height of summer heat stress. If you only want to increase the humidity, install mist nozzles rather than sprinklers.

A drip irrigation system applies water slowly through emitters or perforated pipes. The most popular systems use a PVC pipe running down the center of the bench to supply water, with microtubes running to each pot. Held in place by stakes or lead weights at their ends, the tubes direct dripping water into each pot. Dry leaves, constant water supply, water conservation, and convenience are the advantages of drip irrigation.

When dry leaves are important for plant health, consider capillary matting to water groups of similar plants. The mat stays wet, and plants take up just what water they need from below. To set up the system, first cover the bench with plastic sheeting. Buy a mat just smaller than the size of the bench; do not let it hang over the edge. Wet the mat by hand, or add a drip hose on a timer to do the job for you at regular intervals.

WATER QUALITY ISSUES

The majority of treated municipal water supplies deliver water suitable for most greenhouse uses. Well or pond water must be tested before use to be sure the pH is neutral and mineral deposits are minimal. Add a 100- to 150-mesh water filter to the line to capture sand and soil particles, algae, and other particulate matter; clean or replace the filter regularly. Many tropical plants, especially those in the lily family, display brown leaf tips in the presence of fluoridated water. Fill your watering can and let it sit several hours before watering such plants, and do not use the bottom inch of water in the can. If you collect rainfall to water plants, test its pH occasionally for safe use.

FERTILIZING SYSTEMS

Optimum plant growth is encouraged when you make fertilizer available to plants in small but frequent doses. Most premium potting mixes contain a well-balanced supply of nutrients to begin with, but all growing media need replenishing as the nutrients are used or leach out over time. You can maintain some foliage plants in good soil with only the addition of timed-release fertilizers several times a year. Nearly all other plants need more nutrition for good health.

Water-soluble fertilizers have nearly replaced granular formulas for greenhouse use because they are so much easier to mix and apply. You can hand-feed by mixing a dilute solution and applying it with a watering can. A safe concentration for use several times a week on most plants mixes the fertilizer at one-fifth the rate recommended for monthly feeding. If the label calls for 1 tablespoon in a gallon of water, mix yours at 1 tablespoon to 5 gallons of water.

Solubles also enable you to water and fertilize at the same time, but the basic rule still applies: Never fertilize a dry pot. If the pots are dry when you want to fertilize, water lightly first, then water again with the fertilizer solution. It is still essential to water the pots thoroughly every other week to leach out harmful buildup of salts. Irrigate with plain water until it runs out the drain holes to exchange gases and remove salts from the soil.

Be sure the soluble fertilizer you choose is a complete formula. Plants need three major nutritional elements for healthy growth—nitrogen (N), phosphorus (P), and potassium (K). Nitrogen promotes green shoots and leaves; without it, new growth is pale or nonexistent. Phosphorus and potassium provide the energy for strong cell walls, flowers, and fruits. Their deficiency shows up as stunted plants, few flowers, and weak or absent fruit. Most greenhouse growers use one evenly balanced formula such as 20-20-20, and another to promote flowering and fruiting such as 5-30-15. Other essential nutrients, required in much smaller amounts, are known as the minor elements. Usually supplied in the balanced fertilizers you use, minor elements can be applied as needed for specific plants.

Popular today with all sorts of busy gardeners, timed-release fertilizers have their nutrients wrapped in varying amounts of soluble coatings. With regular watering, the coatings are washed away and their nutrients are released. Some growers apply a half-dose to every pot in the greenhouse as insurance against human error so the plants always have some nutrients available.

AUTOMATED FERTILIZING SYSTEMS

Because their roots are restricted in containers, plants in a greenhouse need more frequent watering and feeding than the same plants in a garden bed. Yet excess water and nutrients can spell disaster for plants on the greenhouse bench. By automating watering systems, you can water and fertilize on a schedule that suits both you and your plants.

Two kinds of partially automated fertilizing systems add convenience to your greenhouse regime. Both are automated in that they deliver a fertilizer solution with water through the hose or other delivery system. But unlike other automated systems, you must mix and monitor the concentrate closely before operating.

Once you get the hang of mixing the solutions, siphon proportioners and fertilizer injectors save time and deliver consistently. The siphon device looks like a double fitting for a water hose with a tube running off it. The tube goes into a bucket of concentrated fertilizer. Attach one end of the siphoner to the faucet and connect the other end to the hose. As you water, fertilizer is sucked up and diluted to a strength safe for the plants.

Some fertilizer injectors use a cartridge or canister to dispense appropriate amounts through drip and sprinkler irrigation systems. Most injectors use a pump operated by water pressure or flow. Look for an injector with an antisiphon valve built in, or attach a separate backflow preventer to the injector.

MIXING CONCENTRATES

Siphon fertilizer injectors add 1 part fertilizer to 15 parts water. Simply translated, that means you must mix the solution 15 times stronger than you want the resulting irrigation water to be. If the label calls for 1 tablespoon to 1 gallon of water, use 15 times that amount—15 tablespoons in 1 gallon of water.

A water-driven fertilizer injector provides readily available, more accurate mixing of soluble plant foods.

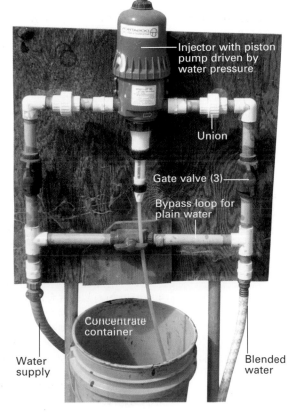

Injector with piston pump driven by water pressure

Union

Gate valve (3)

Bypass loop for plain water

Concentrate container

Water supply

Blended water

MANAGING THE GREENHOUSE

Floors and benches filled with gravel absorb heat all day and release it overnight to help maintain the warm greenhouse conditions needed to grow most cacti and succulents.

When you build a greenhouse, you are only setting the stage. The real show lies in how you manage the environment. The three big factors that you control are temperature, humidity, and light. After you provide soil, fertilizer, and water to sustain plants, you employ cultural techniques that encourage continued growth. This chapter explains these crucial factors and offers ways to manipulate them to advantage.

THE POWER OF MODERATION

Perhaps the greatest joy of greenhouse gardening is the impact it can have on your daily life. In this world where the day's activities seem to rush people from place to place, the greenhouse stands waiting to welcome you home.

The hallmark of good greenhouse management is moderation and consistency, and you establish that condition with your daily routine. The health of your plants depends on the regimen you set. Plants thrive when watered and fertilized regularly, inspected daily for growth and pests, and when the greenhouse structure is kept in good repair. If you wait until it freezes to turn on the heat, don't water plants until they wilt, or let the greenhouse drip with condensation before venting, you create stressful conditions for plants—and more work for yourself in nursing plants back to health.

A five-minute walk through the greenhouse at least once every day can help you notice problems before they become a crisis. For most gardeners, that daily survey is one of life's greatest joys. As you create good habits that develop into a familiar routine, managing your greenhouse will become easy, natural, and rewarding.

MANAGING TEMPERATURE

Temperature—of the air, soil, and water—plays a huge role in plant growth. As with other factors, the key is moderation. Greenhouse design and practices determine your control over air temperature; it must stay in the range required by your plants. Soil temperature is even more critical for most plants, which is why root zone heating is becoming popular with commercial growers. If water feels cold to your hand, it can cause leaf spots on susceptible seedlings and plants. Let it stand until tepid in a watering can, or warm the hose in sunlight before using. However, water overheated by sun warming the hose can burn leaves, so let the first blast run out before watering pots. If air and water temperatures remain moderate, soil temperatures will, too.

When you keep the greenhouse too warm, plants tend to have smaller leaves and blossoms, paler color, and distorted stems with elongated nodes. Because warmer temperatures cause plants to lose water faster through their leaves and more rapidly use up whatever water is available to the roots, wilting occurs. Cold temperatures can encourage flowering in some plants; you put this quality to work when you force bulbs to bloom. Temperatures that are too cold cause plant growth to slow or even stop. Plants wilt and colors are distorted.

Moderating temperatures in the greenhouse can be as simple as keeping tabs on the thermometer, or as complex as maintaining the heat and vent systems, checking the temperature day and night, and providing additional insulation and shade when necessary. If cold water will be a consistent problem, consider adding a heater to the greenhouse water line.

TEMPERATURE RANGES

Each plant species has an acceptable temperature range that relates to its native environment. Alpines that evolved to withstand frozen soil for months do not grow in the tropics, for example.

Over time some plants can adapt to changing conditions; others never do. Some people build a greenhouse specifically to grow tropical plants and know they should maintain a minimum temperature of 60 degrees F, with daytime highs ideally not greater than 85 degrees. That can be expensive, so after the first season they lower the minimum temperature 5 degrees to save money. Many of the plants readily adapt; others can be located on the warmest bench or in a plastic tent during cold weather.

The majority of greenhouse gardeners maintain a moderate temperature range because it is economical to operate. Many plants native to temperate zones thrive in it, as well as subtropical foliage and flowering houseplants, most warm-weather vegetables, and many bulbs. All prefer a daytime temperature between 55 and 70 degrees F. Nights can be as low as 50 degrees F with no noticeable effect, but if daytime temperatures stay above 80 degrees F consistently, most plants suffer.

A cool-range greenhouse maintains a temperature of 45 degrees F that can range up to 60 degrees F on a sunny day. This is the least expensive type of greenhouse to heat, often at one-third the cost of the moderate-temperature greenhouse. You can overwinter tender plants, maintain propagated shrubs, and grow cool-weather vegetables.

Many orchids prefer a greenhouse with moderate temperatures. Be prudent about ventilation to keep temperatures and humidity within the desired range. Consider adding a fan at bench level.

Plants that favor cool conditions are excellent candidates for a solar greenhouse with minimal supplemental heat.

MANAGING LIGHT AND HUMIDITY

Measure light in the greenhouse in at least three places, then match the plants' locations to their needs. Take separate readings at ground level, on the bench, and above it on shelves and hangers that hold plants.

All green plants need light, but the intensity and duration needs differ from one species to another. In general, flowering plants need twice as much light as those grown for their leaves.

Light is the visible portion of the electromagnetic spectrum. It is a blend of red, orange, yellow, green, blue, and violet rays. Plants absorb primarily the blue and red rays; blue promotes leaf maturity and red affects flowering and other growth processes. Plants reflect green and yellow light; that's why they display those colors to the human eye.

The critical qualities for greenhouse light are how much the plants receive (intensity) and how long it lasts (duration). Intensity is determined by the strength of the light source itself and its distance from the plants. Light is measured in foot-candles or lumens, depending on whether you are considering the lit object or the light source. Light that falls on the plant is calculated in foot-candles; the light source itself is rated in lumens, as is given on a lightbulb box.

One foot-candle is the amount of visible light falling on 1 square foot of surface located 1 foot away from a source of one lumen (usually a 10-inch taper). You can probably read a newspaper in about 20 foot-candles, but it takes more than that to grow plants. Use the light meter in a camera to test the light in any area. Set the film-speed dial to ASA 25 and shutter speed to ⅟₆₀ second. Put a sheet of white paper where you want to measure light, focus the camera on the paper, and adjust the f-stop until you could take a photograph. Use the chart below to translate f-stop settings into foot-candles.

Day length, or how long the light hits your plants, plays an especially big role in flowering. By manipulating light and dark, you can duplicate the natural cycle of plants and force blooming at any time of the year. Flowering in some plants is triggered by long days and short nights (usually six to 10 hours of darkness). This group includes petunia, snapdragon, bromeliads, azalea, and hibiscus. Others bloom in response to short days and long nights, such as chrysanthemums, fuchsia, gardenia,

SUPPLEMENTAL LIGHTING OPTIONS

INCANDESCENT BULBS: Although they can be used as a source of heat in a limited area, incandescents are inefficient for providing light for plants, and are seldom used alone for supplemental light.

FLUORESCENT GROW-LIGHTS: Use spot or tube lamps on a timer to supplement sunlight and grow seedlings in winter.

COMBINATION OF FLUORESCENTS: To achieve the full spectrum, use one daylight and one cool white fluorescent tube in a dual fixture. Cool white fluorescents are even more efficient than grow-lights at providing supplemental light for plants.

COMBINATION OF INCANDESCENT AND FLUORESCENT: Use in a greenhouse with less than six hours of sunlight per day in the growing season.

HIGH-PRESSURE SODIUM AND METAL HALIDE: About one-third more efficient than fluorescent, they are available in wattages that fit hobby greenhouse use.

TRANSLATE F-STOP INTO FOOT-CANDLES

F-Stop Setting	Foot-Candles	Appropriate Plants
2	100	Chinese evergreen, cast-iron plant, green pothos, heart-leaf philodendron
2.8	200	Variegated pothos, dumb cane, rubber tree, fern
4	370	Fiddle-leaf fig, prayer plant, Swedish ivy, variegated dumb cane
5.6	750	Most seedlings, flowering bulbs
8	1,500	Orchids, mums, roses, succulents
11	2,800	Leafy vegetables, citrus
16	5,000	Fruits and vegetables, cacti

poinsettia, and many orchids. You can control the amount of light available to your plants.

Lengthening the day for plants is one use of supplemental light sources in the greenhouse. If your greenhouse receives less than six hours of direct sunlight each day, you may need to supplement sunlight with artificial light to grow most plants year-round.

You can reduce day length by excluding light on a schedule—a technique sometimes necessary to initiate blooming for certain plants. Build a simple frame to hold black cloth (not plastic) above the pots on the bench—use big utility clamps or screws to attach side pieces of PVC pipe or wood, then string clothesline wire to support the cloth. Raise the cloth at least 4 inches over the plants to maintain air circulation around them, and remember to remove the cloth and then re-cover the plants daily.

IMPORTANCE OF HUMIDITY

When humidity in the greenhouse stays below 50 percent for long periods, plant growth suffers, because leaves lose water faster than they can replace it. Likewise, if humidity soaks the air at 80 percent or greater for any length of time, the risk of leaf diseases increases. Maintaining humidity levels somewhere in between is crucial to growing healthy plants. Methods to moderate humidity differ depending on your needs and available equipment.

Low humidity can be an ongoing challenge, especially in arid regions and for tropical species grown in temperate climates. Simply misting the plants or watering the floor two or three times a day usually works. An evaporative cooling system adds humidity to the air, as does a humidifier.

If you live in an arid region where you must fight high temperatures and low humidity much of the year, consider a mist system. Just like the smaller version used to propagate plants, the greenhouse system needs only a water source and timer. You can run a pipe along the ridge or down the sides of the benches. Set up two timers: one to turn the system on during the day and off at night, and another to run the spray nozzles every few minutes when the system is on. Set the timing sequence yourself, to be sure your plants are misted only when the humidity reaches a certain minimum. Depending on your conditions, this could be twice every 10 minutes or once each half-hour.

For water conservation and to prevent overwatering, look for mist controls that shut off as water builds up on the monitor. The problem with timer-operated controls is that they mist or water by the clock you set, not according to the plants' needs. On overcast days, less water evaporates from leaves, and they can get too wet with an automatic mister. Other systems that provide good control include those governed by humidistat- and light-activated interval switches.

Most greenhouse gardeners want to grow at least a few tropical plants, but other favorites may suffer and die in the high humidity. Most plants do well with a relative humidity from 50 percent to 70 percent, but many tropical plants prefer 80 percent. Create a microclimate around those philodendrons, dumb canes, and false aralias to meet their special needs. Put a tray of pebbles under pots, or group larger pots in a contained area of the gravel floor. Nestle 2×4s in the gravel to make a floor tray. Place a tent of plastic film over each plant, held 3 to 4 inches above the leaves by a frame of PVC. Add water daily and keep the level just below the top of the rocks so no roots sit in the water. The constant evaporation of the water raises the humidity around the plants, slowing down the loss of water through the leaves.

Either install a fluorescent fixture on chains to raise and lower it, or elevate flats of seedlings to within 4 inches of the light. Lower the seedlings as they grow taller.

REDUCING HUMIDITY

Some plant diseases thrive in a moist environment. Water vapor from the air will condense on plant surfaces if the plant is cooler than the air. This can lead to the growth of pathogens.

High-humidity conditions are most common during spring and fall. During summer the temperature stays warm all night, and during winter the heating system is operating and drying out the air. The humidity increases as the temperature in the greenhouse decreases during the late afternoon and may stay high all night.

Ventilation is the best way to control high humidity. The air outside is drier than the inside air. (Adding heat to the air increases its moisture-holding capacity.) The cost of the heat used is less than 1 cent each time the greenhouse volume is changed. This may have to be done several times to dry out a saturated greenhouse. Cracking the vent open or turning on the fan for a minute will do the job.

GOOD CULTURAL PRACTICES

Good greenhouse growing techniques encourage healthy plant growth. By providing the appropriate light, temperature, and moisture, then irrigating and fertilizing regularly, you ensure healthy plants that are less vulnerable to pests.

Consistent care contributes to the moderate environment you set up in the greenhouse. If you water erratically and the growing space heats up during the day, humidity may be inadequate and your plants will become stressed. Water earlier in the day rather than later, returning in late afternoon if needed during hot weather but still early enough for surfaces to dry out before nightfall.

Plan ahead to seed, root, transplant, graft, fertilize, cut back, and divide each group of plants. Arrange the crops in groups and note on your calendar which gets what and when. Use the calendar on pages 76 and 77 to guide you in scheduling tasks. Some growers put a chalkboard in the potting shed, others a wall calendar. Once you have established a routine that works for you and your plants, keep it going.

GOOD SANITATION

The first line of defense against nearly all greenhouse plant problems is good sanitation. Take regular measures to maintain a clean, healthy environment. Any clutter that takes up space, absorbs light, or collects stagnant water works against cleanliness. Don't leave hose nozzles dripping, and clean and put away flats, bags of soil, and tools after using. Store flats, pots, and tools away from the growing space. Provide a hook or reel and keep water hoses and nozzles coiled up so they stay clean and you don't trip over them. Insects and disease pathogens can breed on damp surfaces; keep them dry. Bags of soil amendments and potting mix should be stored in bins with tight-fitting lids. Fertilizers, pesticides, and other chemicals should be stored in airtight, leakproof containers and kept in a locked cabinet.

Give each pot enough space on the greenhouse bench. Air circulation among pots is important for healthy, symmetrical growth. Insects can crawl from plant to plant and fungi can spread more easily when leaves touch. Water standing in saucers or draining from one plant to another is not desirable.

Smart sanitation practice extends to the plants themselves. Remove old leaves and flowers and wash the leaves to clean them regularly. Isolate any plants you are treating for pests to prevent contaminating other plants. And no matter how sentimentally attached you are, get rid of plants that simply cannot be rid of insects or cured of fungal diseases. Take cuttings to keep the plants going. When a flat of seedlings damps off, discard the plants immediately and replace the soil and container before replanting.

Before starting on your first project, and at least annually, you are well-advised to sterilize the greenhouse interior. Take the plants outside or cover them. Then make a bucket full of bleach solution (1 part bleach to 9 parts water), don gloves and old clothes, and use a broom or mop to wash all the interior surfaces. Scrub every nook and cranny, then air the place out completely before putting the plants back.

SOLVING PEST PROBLEMS

The first line of defense against pests is your greenhouse door. Don't purchase a plant with apparent pest damage; inspect each before you buy it. Isolate new plants for a week to 10 days before adding them to the bench. If it is impractical to leave them outside, set up a plastic isolation tent inside.

Walk through the greenhouse every day with a vigilant eye for the first chewed leaf or rotten stem. Put up an insect trap such as a yellow sticky card so you know when flying insects appear. When you see a chewed leaf, look for the culprit, then destroy it. Know that a lone intruder is unlikely; check that plant and the ones around it daily.

Once you identify a problem you want to tackle, do so actively but incrementally. Set the plant(s) apart on the bench, cut off and throw away the damaged parts, and watch the plant carefully. Unless the leaves are fragile, force insects off with a water stream, then watch to see if they return over a few days. All but the hairiest leaves can be washed with a solution of 1 tablespoon of pure soap in 2 quarts of water, then rinsed with clean water.

Isolating new arrivals for a week before introducing them to the greenhouse bench gives hitchhiking insects a chance to hatch so you can readily control them.

Sticky traps attract the first flying insects to arrive. Your vigilance in controlling those primary pests can prevent wholesale infestation later.

SOLVING CULTURAL PROBLEMS

Knowing the special needs of particular plants can help prevent problems caused by the way you care for them. The way you water makes a big difference, as can other cultural practices that both cause and solve common problems. You should employ cultural strategies to postpone or defeat inevitable pest problems. This section will help you identify and solve common greenhouse plant problems.

WATER SPOTS

PROBLEM: White to light yellow blotches in various patterns, including circles, occur on the older leaves. Small islands of green may be separated by the discolored areas. Brown spots sometimes appear in the colored areas.

VULNERABLE PLANTS: Hairy-leaved tropical plants, especially members of the African violet family such as *Saintpaulia* (African violet), *Gloxinia*, *Streptocarpus*, and *Achimenes*.

ANALYSIS: Some plants are very sensitive to rapid temperature changes. Water spots occur most commonly when cold water is splashed on the leaves during watering.

SOLUTION: Fill a can with water and let it stand until it feels tepid to your finger, then water. Grow problem plants in reservoir pots, water pots from below, use wick systems, or use drip irrigation. Spotted leaves will not recover. Pick off unsightly leaves.

SALT DAMAGE

PROBLEM: The leaf margins of plants with broad leaves or the leaf tips of plants with long, narrow leaves turn dark brown and die. This browning occurs on the older leaves first, but when the condition is severe, new leaves may also be affected. Plants may be stunted, with brittle leaves curling downward. On some plants, older leaves may yellow and die. Crusty, lumpy white or tan sediment forms on the edges of pots or the surface of the soil.

VULNERABLE PLANTS: All container plants fertilized frequently, especially those in clay pots, those with attached saucers, and those irrigated by drip systems only.

ANALYSIS: Roots pick up soluble salts, which accumulate in the margins and tips of leaves. When concentrations become high, the tissues are killed. Salts can accumulate from water or the use of fertilizers, or they may be present in the soil used in potting.

SOLUTION: Leach excess salts from soil by flushing with water. Water thoroughly at least three times, letting water drain from the pot each time. Never let a plant stand in drainage water. Prevent by leaching twice a month.

NITROGEN DEFICIENCY

PROBLEM: Oldest leaves turn yellow and may drop. Yellowing starts at the leaf margins and progresses inward without producing a distinct pattern. Growth is slow, new leaves are small, and plants may be stunted.

VULNERABLE PLANTS: All plants.

ANALYSIS: Plants use nitrogen in large amounts. When there is not enough, it is taken from older leaves for use in new growth. Nitrogen is easily leached from soil by watering.

SOLUTION: Establish a regular program of applying a balanced fertilizer containing sufficient quantities of nitrogen. A solution of water-soluble fertilizer provides a rapid-acting source.

IRON DEFICIENCY

PROBLEM: Newer leaves turn yellow from the margins inward while veins remain green. The plant may be stunted.

VULNERABLE PLANTS: Acid-loving plants, such as *Gardenia*, *Rhododendron*, and *Citrus*.

ANALYSIS: A common problem with plants that grow best in soil with a pH between 5.5 and 6.5. When the soil pH is above 7.0, iron is found in a less soluble form that is not available to some plants. Waterlogged soil can also result in symptoms.

SOLUTION: Spray foliage with a chelated iron fertilizer, and apply the fertilizer to the soil in the pot. In the future, fertilize with a plant food formulated for acid-loving plants. Use an acidic soil mix that contains at least 50 percent peat moss. Be sure that the soil is well-drained.

Water spots on African violet

Nitrogen deficiency in Citrus

Salt burn on Dieffenbachia

Iron deficiency in Gardenia

SOLVING CULTURAL PROBLEMS
continued

UNDER- OR OVERWATERING

PROBLEM: Underwatering—Plant parts or whole plants wilt but recover with irrigation. Margins or tips of leaves may dry and become brittle but still retain a dull green color. Areas between the veins may bleach and turn tan or brown. Flowers drop off. Plants may become stunted, stop growing, or die.

Overwatering—Plants wilt and do not recover with irrigation; leaves lose their glossiness, turn yellow, and drop off. The roots are brown and soft and do not have white tips. The soil in the bottom of the pot may be wet and have a foul odor. Plants may die.

VULNERABLE PLANTS: All plants.

ANALYSIS: Water makes up most of the tissue of plants and is the medium that carries nutrients into the plant. A plant that is frequently short of water is also short of nutrients. Water also cools the leaves as it evaporates. If a leaf has no water to evaporate, it may overheat in the sun and burn.

Although plants need water, roots also need air. If soil is kept too wet, air spaces are filled with water and the roots are weakened and susceptible to rot and may die. Diseased roots do not absorb water well, so the soil remains wet. Damaged roots cannot pick up water and nutrients needed for growth.

SOLUTION: Underwatering—Water plants immediately and thoroughly. If the soil is completely dry, soak the entire pot in water for a couple of hours. Monitor automatic systems closely. Most plants need water when the top inch of soil feels dry to the touch.

Overwatering—Prevent the problem by using light soil with good drainage. Make sure containers drain well and roots do not stand in water. Repot affected plants into smaller pots until roots regrow. Clean pots before reuse. Do not water less severely affected plants until the soil is barely moist. Discard severely wilted plants and those without white root tips.

Far Right: Overwatering damage to Schefflera. If you suspect overwatering damage, lift the plant from its pot and inspect the roots. Be sure to provide good drainage for all plants grown in containers.

TOO LITTLE OR TOO MUCH LIGHT

PROBLEM: Too little light—Stems and leafstalks may elongate and be spindly and weak. Plants lean toward a light source. Leaves may be lighter green and smaller than normal. Lobes and splits that are normal in leaves may fail to develop. Lower leaves may yellow and drop. On some plants, leaves at first are larger and thinner than normal, then are smaller than normal. Flowering plants fail to produce flowers, and plants with colorful foliage become pale. Variegated plants may lose their variegation and become green. Plants stretch, growing too much stem between each new set of leaves. Stems grow thin and pale. New shoots wilt.

Too much light—Dead tan or brown patches may develop on leaves that are exposed to direct sunlight, or leaf tissue may lighten or turn gray. In some cases, the plant remains green but growth is stunted. Damage is most severe when the plant is allowed to dry out. Flowers open too rapidly, are small, and feel papery.

VULNERABLE PLANTS: All greenhouse plants, especially right after being moved up to the bench (too much light) or in from outdoors (too little light).

ANALYSIS: Plant cells grow properly only with adequate light. Their size, growth rate, and configuration are directly related to their exposure. Given too much or too little sun or artificial light, the plants exhibit distorted growth. A change in available sunlight due to pot placement in the greenhouse, abrupt removal of shade, or the higher angle of the summer sun can be the cause.

SOLUTION: Place plants appropriately, then keep a careful eye on their performance and move them when necessary to increase or decrease light exposure. Move plants gradually, changing their exposure in small steps. Adjust height of artificial light sources.

Sunburn on Dieffenbachia. Sun-scorched leaves dehydrate until individual cells collapse. Although this leaf will not recover, sun scorch seldom kills a plant if handled right away.

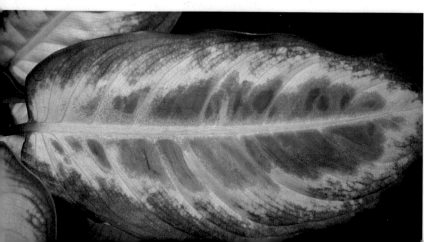

SOLVING PEST PROBLEMS

*Slug and snail damage on young **Delphinium** plants. Each hole in a leaf represents a loss to that plant both in its looks and its viability.*

SNAILS AND SLUGS

PROBLEM: Holes appear in healthy leaves, new growth tips are chewed off, or entire leaves may be sheared from the stem. Seedlings are sheared off and eaten, with only the stems emerging from the ground. Silvery trails may wind around on leaves, soil, pots, or bench tops. Snails or slugs may be seen moving around or feeding on plants, especially at night.

VULNERABLE PLANTS: Newly transplanted seedlings, fleshy leaved plants, and any plants with new growth close to soil level.

ANALYSIS: Like most mollusks, snails and slugs need to be moist all the time; they avoid direct sun and dry places and hide during the day in damp places, such as under flowerpots or in thick ground covers, moist soil, and gravel. They emerge at night or on cloudy days to feed. Slugs lay white eggs encased in a slimy mass in protected places. Snails bury their eggs in the soil, also in a slimy mass.

SOLUTION: Isolate new plants before introducing them to the bench. Inspect all plants and their surroundings regularly, especially at night. Plug leaks and close doors. Hand-pick and destroy the first invaders. For severe infestations, repot plants, discarding the old soil, and dry out the environment. For chemical treatment, scatter granular snail and slug killer in bands around the areas you wish to protect. Also scatter the bait in areas where snails or slugs might be hiding, such as in dense ground covers, compost piles, or pot storage areas. Before spreading the bait, wet down the treated areas to encourage snail and slug activity that night. Repeat the application every two weeks for as long as snails and slugs are active.

WHITEFLIES AND THRIPS

PROBLEM: Whiteflies—Tiny white-winged adults feed mainly on the undersides of leaves; nonflying, scalelike larvae the size of a pinhead covered with waxy, white powder may also be present on the undersides of leaves. The upper surfaces of leaves appear stippled with tiny white or yellow spots; leaves may be covered with a sticky substance that turns black with sooty mold, a secondary fungus. When the plant is touched, insects flutter rapidly around it.

Greenhouse thrips—Leaves become silvery or bleached. Damaged leaves wilt, become papery, and usually drop prematurely. Tiny (1/20-inch) black insects may be observed feeding on the inner parts of the north side of a plant, where large colonies leave quantities of varnishlike black spots.

VULNERABLE PLANTS: Nearly all greenhouse plants, but especially those with relatively thin leaves, including roses, poinsettias, herbs, and chrysanthemums.

ANALYSIS: Whiteflies and greenhouse thrips pierce and suck greenhouse plants. The damage is easy to overlook initially, but the overall effect on plants is severe dehydration. Feeding may also transmit plant viruses. Both kinds of insects enter the greenhouse through unscreened windows and vents, on newly acquired plants, and on plants grown outdoors in summer and brought into the greenhouse for the winter.

SOLUTION: Carefully isolate and observe all plants before introducing or reintroducing them to the greenhouse, and use thrips screening on windows and vents. To control both insects, remove all heavily infested leaves. Vacuum plants to pick up adults. To chemically control whiteflies on ornamentals (not food crops), spray plants with a systemic insecticide containing *acephate* at least three times at intervals of four to six days. Whiteflies may also be partially controlled with yellow sticky traps; place yellow sticky stakes upright in each container. To chemically control greenhouse thrips on ornamentals, spray plants with an insecticide containing *acephate*, *bifenthrin*, or *malathion*.

Whiteflies seldom arrive on your plants as adults, but wingless white nymphs soon develop into mobile pests unless they are controlled quickly.

SOLVING PEST PROBLEMS
continued

MEALYBUGS, SCALE INSECTS, AND APHIDS

PROBLEM: Mealybugs—Cottony or waxy white insects are on the undersides of leaves, on stems, and particularly in crotches or where leaves are attached. Cottony masses that contain eggs of the insects may also be present. Plants do not grow well and may die.

Scale—Nodes, stems, and leaves are covered with cottony, cushionlike white masses; crusty brown bumps; or clusters of somewhat flattened, scaly reddish, gray, or brown bumps. Leaves turn yellow and may drop off.

Aphids—Tiny (⅛-inch) nonwinged, soft-bodied green insects cluster on buds, young stems, and leaves. Leaves are curled, discolored, and reduced in size.

All three insects produce a sticky substance that may cover the leaves or drop onto surfaces below the plant. Black sooty mold can grow on the sticky substance.

VULNERABLE PLANTS: All plants.

ANALYSIS: Mealybugs, scale insects, and aphids are piercing and sucking insects that feed on plant sap. Although they do little damage in small numbers, populations can rapidly build up to devastate plants. Aphids may spread viruses to susceptible plants.

SOLUTION: Inspect new plants thoroughly before putting them in the greenhouse. At first sign, isolate affected plants with a plastic drop between them and the rest of the bench. Wash each plant with soapy water, let dry thoroughly, then paint each stem with rubbing alcohol. Carefully check all parts of the plant to make sure all insects have been removed. Search for mealybug egg sacs under the rims or bottoms of pots, in cracks or on the undersides of shelves and benches, and on brackets and plant hangers. Wipe off any sacs. Discard severely infested plants, and avoid taking cuttings from such plants. Thoroughly clean the growing area with soapy water before starting new plants. For chemical control, apply an insecticidal soap spray containing *pyrethrin*, or a systemic insecticide containing *acephate* or *bifenthrin*.

Several female citrus mealybugs feed on coleus near an egg sac that has been deposited in a typical location: the junction of stems.

SPIDER MITES

PROBLEM: Leaves are stippled, yellowing, and dirty. Leaves may dry out and drop. There may be webbing over flower buds, between leaves, on the growing points of shoots, and/or on the lower surfaces of leaves. To determine if a plant is infested with mites, examine the bottoms of the leaves with a hand lens. Or hold a sheet of white paper underneath a suspicious leaf and tap the leaf sharply. Mites look like minute specks the size of pepper grains that drop to the paper and begin to crawl around. The pests are easily seen against the white background.

VULNERABLE PLANTS: Most greenhouse plants are susceptible, but perennials and woody plants as well as African violets seem to be particularly vulnerable hosts.

ANALYSIS: These mites, related to spiders, are major greenhouse pests. They cause damage by sucking sap from the undersides of leaves. Under warm, dry conditions, mites can build up to tremendous numbers. The use of only drip emitters to water, as well as excessively hot and dry or low humidity conditions encourage spider mites.

SOLUTION: Avoid introducing infested plants into the greenhouse. Prevent hot and dry greenhouse conditions. Maintain minimum recommended humidity levels, even with drip irrigation, by installing misters. When watering by hand, be sure to wet the undersides of leaves weekly. Once symptoms develop, isolate infested plants. Cut away and discard damaged parts. Wash mites off the remaining leaves with a strong spray of water. Discard seriously infested plants. For chemical control, apply a systemic insecticide containing *acephate* or *bifenthrin*.

Suspect spider mites on leaves dehydrated for no apparent reason. Some species spin a thin web you can feel, or the mites may be visible as tiny red specks. Should your spider mite infestation be as pronounced as this one, throw the plants away; do not compost them.

SOLVING DISEASE PROBLEMS

RUST

PROBLEM: Yellow or orange spots appear on the upper surfaces of leaves. Yellowish-orange, rust, or chocolate-colored pustules of spores develop on the undersides of leaves. Infected leaves usually dry up and die. The plant may be stunted.

VULNERABLE PLANTS: Roses, geraniums, many bedding annuals, vegetables, and fruits.

ANALYSIS: Rust is a plant disease caused by any of several related fungi. Most rust fungi undergo a dormant stage as spores on living plant tissue and, in some cases, in plant debris. Some rust fungi also infect various weeds and woody trees and shrubs during part of their life cycle. Splashing water and moving air spread the spores to healthy plants. Some rust fungi cannot infect their host unless the foliage is wet for six to eight hours. Rust is favored by moist conditions, cool nights, and warm days.

SOLUTION: Several different fungicides are used to control rust, depending on the species of the host plant. Consult product labels to see if your plants are listed. Spray plants thoroughly at the first sign of disease, covering both the upper and lower surfaces of the leaves. Some plants are so susceptible to rust that you may need to spray at weekly intervals throughout the growing season. Fungicides will protect only uninfected tissues; they will not cure diseased leaves. Allow wet foliage to dry quickly by watering in the morning rather than in the late afternoon or evening. Remove and destroy all severely infected plants. Plant rust-resistant varieties, if available.

Rust spore pustules on the lower surface of a **Pelargonium** *leaf. Rust is a fungal disease that is most active when conditions are moist and humid, nights are cool, and days are warm.*

POWDERY MILDEW

PROBLEM: Powdery, grayish-white spots and patches cover leaves, stems, and flowers, often primarily the upper surfaces of leaves. Infected leaves eventually turn yellow. Whole branches or plants may die.

VULNERABLE PLANTS: Nearly all plants are susceptible to powdery mildew under conditions favorable for the disease. Plants stressed by poor nutrition and drought are often the most attacked.

ANALYSIS: Powdery mildews are plant diseases caused by several closely related fungi that thrive in both humid and dry weather. The powdery patches consist of fungal strands and spores. The spores are spread by moving air to healthy plants. The fungus saps plant nutrients, causing the leaves to turn yellow and sometimes die. A severe infection may kill the plant. The fungus from a diseased plant may infect many other types of plants. Under favorable conditions, powdery mildew can spread through a closely spaced planting in a matter of days. In late summer and fall, the fungus forms small black spore-producing bodies, which remain dormant during winter but can infect more plants the next spring. Powdery mildew is generally most severe in late summer and under humid conditions, although it can also be active during dry weather. Unlike other fungal diseases, which infect only wet leaves, powdery mildew invades dry as well as wet leaves.

SOLUTION: Several different fungicides are used to control powdery mildew. Consult product labels to see if your plant is listed. Spray at regular intervals of 10 to 14 days or as often as necessary to protect new growth. Remove and destroy severely infected plants. Where practical, pick off diseased leaves. Clean up and destroy plant debris. Provide good air circulation and place plants in areas that receive early-morning sun.

Powdery mildew on **Begonia.** *There are many related fungi that cause powdery mildew. Nearly all plants are susceptible if conditions are right.*

SOLVING DISEASE PROBLEMS
continued

GRAY MOLD

PROBLEM: Tiny brown spots appear on blossoms, leaves, and possibly stems. As the disease progresses, spotting increases, and a fuzzy brown or grayish mold forms on the infected tissue. Gray mold and spots often appear on the flowers, especially during cool, wet conditions. The leaves and stems may be soft and rotted.

VULNERABLE PLANTS: Many greenhouse plants, especially those grown for flowers and fruit, including *Cyclamen, Begonia, Cymbidium, Petunia, Gerbera, Pelargonium,* grapes, and strawberries.

ANALYSIS: This widespread plant disease is caused by a genus of fungus (*Botrytis* spp.) that is found on most dead plant tissue. The fungus initially attacks foliage and flowers that are weak or dead, causing spotting and mold. The fuzzy mold that develops is composed of millions of microscopic dark spores. Once gray mold has become established on plant debris and weak or dying leaves and flowers, it can invade healthy plant tissue. The fungus is spread by splashing water and by bits of infected plant debris that land on the leaves. Cool temperatures, moisture, and high humidity promote the growth of gray mold. Crowded plantings and overhead watering also enhance its spread. In the moderate temperature of the greenhouse, gray mold can be a year-round problem.

SOLUTION: Practice good greenhouse sanitation: Clean up plant debris, remove it from the greenhouse, and destroy it. Remove and destroy dying or infected leaves, stems, and flowers at the first sign of infection. Provide enough space between plants to allow good air circulation, and vent more often. Try to avoid wetting the foliage when watering. Control gray mold with a fungicide containing *chlorothalonil* (Daconil 2787®) or *mancozeb*. Spray every one to two weeks as long as the mold is visible.

Excessive humidity in a greenhouse can promote fungal diseases such as the gray mold on this petunia. The disease can spread rapidly.

DAMPING-OFF; ROOT ROT

PROBLEM: Seedlings die overnight soon after emerging from the soil and are found lying on the soil surface. Stems are black and shrunken at soil level. Sometimes seedlings fail to emerge altogether. In older plants, wilting may start on lower leaves and progress gradually up the plant until all the leaves are limp, or it may occur rapidly. Lower leaves and stems often rot. When the plant is pulled out of the ground, the roots are found to be very dark and sometimes badly rotted.

VULNERABLE PLANTS: All germinating seedlings. Among more mature plants, those that grow in clumps or rosettes tend to be most vulnerable.

ANALYSIS: This disease is caused by fungi (*Rhizoctonia* and *Pythium* spp.) that are present in most garden soils. These fungi can live for several years on organic matter in the soil. They thrive in moist, fertile conditions. *Pythium* prefers heavy, poorly aerated soil; *Rhizoctonia* favors aerated, well-drained soil. In seedlings this disease is called damping-off; it thrives in wet, cool soil with a high nitrogen level. In more mature plants it is called root and stem rot. The fungi initially attack the main stem at the soil line or the root system, stunting the plant and causing it to wilt. They then move into the stems and lower leaves, causing rot and eventual death.

SOLUTION: Use sterile seed-starting soil mix and new flats to start seedlings. Purchase seeds treated with a registered fungicide, or protect seeds during germination by coating them with a fungicide containing *captan* or *thiram*. Add a pinch of fungicide to a packet of seeds (or ½ teaspoon per pound), and shake well to coat the seeds with the fungicide. Keep the seed-starting mix warm. Allow the soil surface to dry slightly between waterings, and wait until the first true leaves appear to apply fertilizer. In older plants with root or stem rot, if all the foliage is wilted it's best to discard the plant and soil. In general, to prevent root rot let plants dry out between waterings and space them well apart. Plant in well-drained soil, and never add soil from the garden to your soil mix.

Seedlings affected by damping-off fungi cannot be salvaged. Throw away these plants, their soil, and even the flats and start anew.

USING PESTICIDES

MIXING AND STORING PESTICIDES

Proper mixing and storage of pesticides are necessary for safety and maximum benefit.
MIXING PESTICIDES: Always read the label carefully before mixing pesticides, and mix according to label directions. Keep a separate set of measuring spoons, cups, stirring rods, and other tools to be used only for mixing and measuring pesticides. Make sure mixing and spraying utensils are clean before using them. Mix only the amount needed for the job. Protect your skin from contact with pesticides by wearing clothing that covers your hands, arms, and legs. Wear goggles and a cap to protect your head and face if the label carries a *warning* or *danger* caution. Immediately wash your hands and face and any other area that may have come in contact with the pesticide with soap and water, and remove clothes that have been contaminated. Wash them in warm water with a strong detergent before wearing them again.
STORING CHEMICALS: Always keep pesticides in their original containers. Do not remove the labels, and keep the containers securely capped. Pesticide storage shelves should be strong, stable, and not too high to reach easily, although they should be out of the reach of children. Pesticides are best stored in a locked, well-ventilated space, out of the sun and away from pilot lights and other open flames or sparks, because the fumes may be flammable. Keep the pesticides dry, and do not let liquid pesticides freeze.

APPLYING PESTICIDES

In order for pesticides to be most effective, they must be properly applied. Open all vents, doors, and windows in the greenhouse, and turn off all sprinkler and misting systems. Choose a calm day when the temperature is below 85 degrees F. Keep children, pets, and anyone else well away from the greenhouse when you are applying pesticides. Wear a hat, gloves, and clothing that covers your arms and legs. If the label advises you to use goggles, a respirator, or a mask to avoid exposure to fumes and particles, then do so.

When spraying, it is important that the plant be thoroughly coated. If the label instructions say *wet thoroughly* or *to the drip point,* apply spray until the plant begins to drip. For thorough coverage, spray the plant from two or three directions and from underneath as well as from above.

INSECTICIDES

Many different types of insecticides are on the market today. Most common insecticides have broad-spectrum activity: They are effective against many different types of plant pests. A few insecticides are selective; control is aimed at only one type or group of insects.

Insecticides are either systemic or nonsystemic. A systemic insecticide is a chemical that is absorbed by the roots, stems, or leaves and is carried with the sap throughout the plant. Any pest that feeds on sap from the treated plant is killed. Systemic insecticides usually remain active in the plant for at least two weeks, protecting the plant from reinfestations. They are applied either as granules to the soil or as sprays or drenches.

Nonsystemic chemicals kill on contact, either by direct contact (the spray is absorbed through the body) or through ingestion as the insect feeds on plant tissue.

The persistence of an insecticide is a measure of how quickly it breaks down in the environment. The persistence of most nonsystemic insecticides ranges from several days to months. The less persistent the insecticide, the shorter the time interval between applications.

Be smart when you spray in the greenhouse: Dress to avoid exposure, spray both sides of the aisle so you pass through the house only once, and leave immediately when done. Allow the greenhouse to vent thoroughly for a few hours before re-entering. Read all labels and follow directions carefully; if the label advises you to wear goggles or a respirator, then do so.

GREENHOUSE MANAGEMENT CALENDAR

WINTER

EARLY WINTER

Plant care	Plant Dutch iris in forcing boxes, tulips and narcissus in pots.
	Tropical foliage: fertilize monthly now until early spring.
	Flowering plants: fertilize two times monthly, or set up constant feeding.
	Pot foliage plant cuttings rooted in fall.
	Give plants as holiday gifts with growing instructions.
Greenhouse maintenance	Temporarily caulk or tape anywhere wind blows in.
	Weatherstrip around all doors, windows, and vents.
	Monitor thermostats; clean connections, cover boxes.
	Add plastic film glaze to glass panes.
	Add insulating barriers along solid walls and solar pits.

LATE WINTER

Plant care	Water at midday to prevent heat loss.
	Put sprouted bulb pots in full sun.
	Inspect traps and control insects.
	Start seedlings of spring annual flowers and vegetables.
	Prune fruit trees and shrubs.
Greenhouse maintenance	Use clear tape to temporarily seal new cracks in coverings.
	Keep floors and paths dry.
	Monitor night-time temperature to be sure heat stays within range.
	Add supplemental heating and sidewall venting as needed.
	Inventory pots and supplies.

SPRING

EARLY SPRING

Plant care	Begin fertilizing tropicals every two weeks.
	Transplant fall perennials and spring annuals to garden.
	Start seedlings of summer annual flowers and vegetables.
	Plant summer bulbs in flats.
	Repot tropical foliage plants; air-layer leggy specimens.
Greenhouse maintenance	Unwrap evaporative cooler and sidewall vents; repair if needed.
	Inspect sump pump; clean out gutters; clean screens.
	Monitor temperature closely to avoid midday heat surges.
	Replace cracked storage containers.
	Space plants on benches and add shelves for air circulation.

LATE SPRING

Plant care	Transplant vegetable seedlings.
	Propagate softwood cuttings.
	Pot offsets of spring perennials.
	Expose tropical foliage to more sun for rapid growth.
	Make leaf cuttings of African violets.
Greenhouse maintenance	Replace insect traps for monitoring in greenhouse.
	Begin using evaporative cooling.
	Repair hoses and connectors; replace if needed.
	Add a rack of hanging pots above to provide shade below.
	Turn off heaters and cover or store.

SUMMER

EARLY SUMMER

Plant care	Take semihardwood cuttings and root under mist.
	Move plants to patio, water those remaining daily.
	Wet paths and sidewalls to increase humidity.
	Transplant heat-loving annuals to garden.
	Pot softwood cuttings as they root.
Greenhouse maintenance	Add shade cloth, shutters, and screens as needed.
	Adjust vent timing to increase air.
	Watch sun's angle and remove sun-blockers (such as tree limbs).
	Wash old pots; disinfect for reuse.
	Open greenhouse doors daily for added venting.

LATE SUMMER

Plant care	Root cuttings or start seeds for winter tomatoes.
	Prepare hardwood cuttings.
	Inspect plants for insects, and spray if needed.
	Begin covering poinsettias to force red bracts.
Greenhouse maintenance	Sanitize structure and benches, including mist chamber.
	Repair, replace, or repaint coverings, benches, and doors.
	Inspect sump pump for algae, and treat if needed.
	Oil hinges on vents and doors.
	Clear greenhouse floor of weeds, and replace gravel if needed.

FALL

EARLY FALL

Plant care	Pot up tender annual flowers to overwinter; cut back by half.
	Take cuttings of overgrown foliage plants; root for gifts.
	Apply a light oil spray on fruit trees.
	Seed lettuce, greens, chives, and parsley for winter salads.
	Pot tomatoes; provide cages or stakes; fertilize weekly.
Greenhouse maintenance	Close evaporative cooler and vents; wrap with plastic outside.
	Inspect heaters: clean out debris; repair connections, fins.
	Inspect motors for vents and plastic inflation.
	Reduce temporary shade: remove whitewash, screens, shutters.

LATE FALL

Plant care	Stop covering poinsettias, and begin weekly fertilization.
	Rejuvenate holiday cacti with more light, water, and fertilizer.
	Pot rooted perennials to grow on.
	Move patio-grown tropicals inside; group by growth rate and light needs.
Greenhouse maintenance	Adjust timers to reduce opening frequency of roof vents.
	Add supplemental lighting, timers.
	Remove shade cloth, repair any tears, and store.
	Clean out mist nozzles and water breakers.
	Repair plastic around rooting chambers.

GROWING PROJECTS

Commercial potting mixes for nearly any kind of greenhouse plant are readily available. One cubic foot of potting mix will fill a container 15 inches in diameter and 12 inches deep.

From the day you move the first pot into the greenhouse, you have growing projects. This chapter guides you as you select growing media, take cuttings, start seeds, and grow food—from dwarf fruit trees to hydroponics. You will learn about 12 different plant groups well-adapted to life in the greenhouse, including their strong points, pitfalls, and cultural requirements. A quartet of master projects completes the chapter. Designed to put your skills to work, they represent what greenhouse gardeners do best: growing plants you cannot buy.

GROWING MEDIA

The best soils for greenhouse plants are growing media that contain no garden (or native mineral) soil at all. Garden soil—even the best topsoil from the garden—compacts too readily and does not hold enough water, nutrients, and air for optimum growth in the confines of a container. Garden soil is also frequently contaminated with weed seeds, insects, and disease-producing organisms.

Years ago many greenhouse owners commonly mixed their own soilless media using a variety of recipes. Recent developments in the manufacture and availability of high-quality, reasonably priced commercial growing media have practically eliminated any advantages that most home greenhouse growers find in mixing their own from individual components. The product of extensive research and testing, today's commercial growing media are highly engineered soils that promote the optimum growth of nearly all kinds of plants grown in the greenhouse. For the highest quality growing media, look for brands that have a good reputation with professional growers.

Few things determine greenhouse gardening success as much as the choice of a good growing medium. It can go by many names—potting soil, soilless mix, container soil, container mix, growing mix, or growing medium. Understanding a few industry-wide terms can help you navigate through the many kinds available. A *standard* mix is a basic potting mix designed to sustain plant growth with few or no enhanced growth capabilities. A *premium* mix includes high-tech additions such as fertilizer systems, wetting agents, and extra water-holding capacity that take a lot of the guesswork out of greenhouse gardening. Check labels carefully; most states require potting mixes to list ingredients in order of volume. Mixes that list only a few ingredients are probably standard mixes. Those that list many are generally premium mixes.

For the greatest success, look for a premium growing mix that has the following qualities:

1. HIGH TOTAL POROSITY: Even the best garden soil that is high in organic matter has, at most, a porosity of 30 percent. In contrast, good premium growing mixes achieve a total porosity of 80 percent or more with a combination of organic matter that soaks up water and nutrients like a sponge, such as sphagnum peat moss, coir pith (processed coconut husk), and composted pine bark; and inorganic materials that increase drainage and resist compaction, such as perlite (extremely light granules of volcanic glass expanded by heat). Some inorganic materials, such as vermiculite (mica expanded by heat) and pumice (ground volcanic rock), absorb water as well as increase drainage.

2. APPROPRIATE DENSITY OR WEIGHT:
For most greenhouse gardening, medium and light soil mixes are best. They have high porosity, are easy to handle, have good rigidity to anchor roots, and are usually heavy enough to prevent pots from toppling. Heavy and medium mixes should be used for tall plants to keep them upright. Light mixes are useful in hanging baskets. Super-light mixes should be reserved for situations where weight is especially critical; they are dry and dusty, and pots require special anchoring to keep plants from toppling. Remember that the weight of a mix is not necessarily related to its porosity. Light mixes high in perlite generally have high porosity, but a cactus mix that is heavy because it has a high proportion of sand can have high porosity, too.

3. APPROPRIATE pH: The pH of the growing medium (the measure of acidity and alkalinity) affects the availability of nutrients to plants. Most plants perform best in a mix that is slightly acidic (pH 5.0–6.5), but some plants, such as azaleas and camellias, prefer a more acid mix. Manufacturers add lime or other substances to adjust the pH of their mix. Always check the label to ensure that the pH of a mix is right for your plants.

4. GOOD WETTABILITY: Oils and waxes that occur naturally in organic materials can cause them to shed water and be difficult to wet thoroughly when they dry out. Good premium mixes include a wetting agent to increase the ability of the mix to absorb water quickly.

5. SUFFICIENT NUTRIENTS: Standard mixes have few or no nutrients and require the addition of fertilizers before planting. Good premium mixes include a wide array of fertilizers (as many as five kinds in one mix) that combine slow-release pellets with fast-acting, water-soluble nutrients at the correct level to promote optimum growth.

6. ABSENCE OF WEED SEEDS, INSECTS, AND DISEASE ORGANISMS:
The sphagnum peat, coir pith, and perlite used in the best premium mixes are inherently low in these contaminants. Soilless mixes should not be sterilized; research shows that the presence of beneficial fungi and bacteria is important for plant vigor and health. If compost is included in growing media, it should be processed to kill weed seeds, insects, and disease organisms without killing beneficial fungi and bacteria— a difficult thing to do except under the rigorous, highly controlled conditions perfected by many commercial manufacturers.

POTTING TIPS

Greenhouse containers come in two basic materials: clay (terra-cotta) and plastic. Both serve to hold soil and roots in place, and each has advantages for both plants and growers. Clay pots make a style statement with a practical edge: Excess moisture evaporates through their sides. If you prefer to water every day, use clay pots to help prevent overwatering. Plastic pots, planting cells, and hanging planters cost less than clay, do not have to be watered as often, and keep root zones cooler. Although most are green or white, look for terra-cotta and other colors to complement leaves and flower tones.

Repotting plants in a mature collection can be an annual project, or it may be needed monthly to accommodate seedlings and cuttings as they increase in size. Mature plants send strong messages when it is past time to repot: Water pours straight through and out the drain, because roots have filled the space; pots crack as roots break through; or top-heavy pots fall over. In general, move up to a pot no more than an inch larger than the present one. Depending on the plant, you may repot several times as seedlings and cuttings grow. Keep top and pot in balance, and use conservative amounts of water and fertilizer to encourage compact new growth.

You can damage plant roots if you rip them when repotting. Although that may serve to root-prune a mature *Schefflera* with good results, it can be fatal to seedlings and plants with few or fine-textured roots. Squeeze planting cells and thin-walled plastic pots to release the roots before sliding out the root ball. Turn larger pots upside down and tap the rim on the greenhouse bench to loosen the soil and roots, then slip off the container. As a last resort, break the pot to remove it. In extreme cases, where roots have grown in a tight circle, slice the root ball on four sides before repotting.

When roots are crowded inside pots, water pours right through without benefit to the plant. If roots appear diseased, dip shears in a solution of 1 part household bleach to 9 parts water before and after pruning the roots of each plant.

MAKING MORE PLANTS

Growing plants from cuttings of stems, leaves, or roots is called vegetative propagation. It produces fast, true replicas of the plant you started with, whereas seedlings may take years to grow or be different genetically. Most plants root easily from cuttings, if you take and treat them right.

Most buds along the stem of a cutting can root and sprout under the right conditions. Hardwood, semihardwood, and softwood cuttings, named for the maturity of the wood you cut, are used to root a variety of woody plants.

Take hardwood cuttings in late fall from the mature wood found midway down stems of deciduous shrubs. Trim several inches off the top to make a cutting 1 foot long. Cut it straight across the top and slanted on the bottom so you know which end is up. Then scratch up a few spots 3 inches from the bottom and rub in some rooting hormone. Bundle up a dozen or so cuttings, tie loosely, and bury them bottom end down in perlite for the winter. Keep them moist, cool, and dark, then pot each one separately in late winter. Evergreens take longer to root but respond to a simpler process. Take 4-inch mature cuttings in fall, dip in hormone, and plant in perlite with bottom heat. Tug on them in about three months; resistance means they've

Propagating plants gives you plenty for your own garden as well as to swap, and share. And each flat in the greenhouse saves money when landscaping.

rooted. If the cuttings pull right up and are black at the bottom, discard them and try again with less or no rooting hormone. Pot and set outdoors until midsummer or fall, then transplant to a permanent location.

Semihardwood is just that: not green but not quite woody either. If the branch tip snaps when you bend it, it's probably too old. If it bends double without breaking, it's too young. In midsummer, bend a few each week until the flexibility is just right. Cut off half of every big leaf on the stem. Root like evergreen hardwood cuttings, but keep the potted cuttings in the greenhouse over one winter and plant out in spring.

Softwood cuttings come from spring's newest growth and root in less than a month. Make 4-inch cuttings from side shoots, strip leaves off the lower half, and root with high humidity and bottom heat. Pot them once, then plant in the garden after another two months.

Herbaceous (leafy) cuttings are taken from green-stemmed plants, usually about 3 to 5 inches long; treat them like softwood cuttings.

Leaf cuttings work best for gesneriads and many succulents—plants with thick, fleshy stems and hairy leaves. Use recently matured leaves; do not mist. Root cuttings are reserved for thin-leaved, deciduous shrubs such as lilac, quince, and spirea, whose top cuttings just shrivel and die. In early spring, dig up part of the plant and cut 4-inch lengths of root from just below ground. Plant them ¼ inch deep in the rooting medium; when shoots emerge in a few weeks, pot them up.

FAVORITE PLANTS AND BEST CUTTING TIMES

SHRUBS
AUTUMN—HARDWOOD: *Ceanothus, Cornus, Hypericum, Ligustrum, Lonicera, Prunus, Salix, Vitis, Weigela*
SUMMER—SEMIHARDWOOD: *Akebia, Buddleia, Camellia, Daphne, Euonymus, Forsythia, Hebe, Ilex, Kerria, Nandina, Rosa, Spiraea*
SPRING—SOFTWOOD: *Abelia, Acer, Caryopteris, Clematis, Fuchsia, Halesia, Magnolia, Syringa, Viburnum*
SPRING—ROOTS: *Chaenomeles, Spiraea, Syringa*

PERENNIALS, ANNUALS, AND TROPICALS
HERBACEOUS (GREEN TIP CUTTINGS): *Begonia* (fibrous), *Chrysanthemum, Impatiens, Pelargonium*
LEAF CUTTINGS: *Begonia, Saintpaulia, Sedum, Sinningia*
EARLY SPRING—ROOT SEGMENTS: *Acanthus, Gaillardia, Papaver, Rudbeckia*
SPRING—BASAL SHOOTS: *Aster, Delphinium, Gypsophila, Kniphofia, Lantana, Lupinus, Monarda, Nicotiana, Phlox, Verbena*
EARLY SUMMER—RHIZOMES: *Bergenia, Campanula, Canna, Helianthus*

STARTING SEEDS

The pleasures of starting seeds cannot be overestimated, and your greenhouse is the perfect place to indulge. New plants, different colors, and offbeat varieties can be yours, but perhaps watching the miracle happen again and again is the greatest reward. Buy seed to be certain of its viability and variety, but remember that those you save from hybrid plants, although perhaps different genetically, may be quite interesting.

GROWING FROM SEED

The majority of annual vegetable and flower seeds sprout easily in a good mix on a warm, bright bench. Although individual demands vary, seeds germinate when they have absorbed enough water to nourish their first roots and shoots. To save space, sow seed in flats, then move tiny seedlings into small pots. Lift out a trowel full or spoonful with soil attached, then use your hands to separate the plants; always handle seedlings by their leaves to avoid damaging delicate stems. In general, seedlings are ready to pot up when they have two sets of true leaves. To lessen root damage in transplanting, sow seed directly in small pots. For even more shock prevention, sow in plantable peat pots.

If you have doubts about viability, place 10 seeds on a wet paper towel until they sprout. If fewer than eight (80 percent) sprout, plant thickly. Otherwise, do not, because thinning out some of the seedlings later will disturb all their precious roots.

Even if you recycle other soils for reuse,

be sure seeding mixes are free of disease. Many growers buy sterile seed-starting mix to avoid soilborne pathogens and reduce the chance of otherwise healthy seedlings collapsing overnight.

If seeds planted in sterile, moist soil with plenty of light do not sprout, bottom heat may be the solution. Place a heating cable in a sand bed, or a greenhouse heating mat below the flats; the difference in germination rates is dramatic.

Once seedlings are up, most grow quickly. Your job is to provide enough light to keep them compact. Seedlings in low light struggle; a plant that begins with thin stems and small leaves never lives up to its potential.

Stretched stems and pale green leaves can be caused by low light, but the latter can also signal a need for fertilizer.

Most seedling mixes contain few nutrients. When the plants have two sets of true leaves, begin adding a soluble fertilizer (20-20-20 or its equivalent) to the water weekly.

WOUNDING AND CHILLING

Some seeds respond to wounding, soaking, and chilling to promote germination. Seeds with hard coats, such as nasturtium and sweet pea, break open several days sooner if they are soaked or wounded before planting. Wound really hard seeds with a small file or metal nail file just enough to scar the coat before soaking. To soften seed coats, put seed in warm (not hot) water, swirl for a minute, then let sit from one to four hours, depending on the size of the seeds.

Cold conditioning is the only way to successfully sprout shrubs, trees, and many alpine species. In general, soak seeds before chilling. Do not freeze; the coldest part of your refrigerator (36 to 40 degrees F) is sufficient to chill most seeds.

EASE OF GERMINATING COMMON SEEDS

EASY IN POTS OR FLATS: black-eyed Susan, cosmos, marigold, spider flower, squash, zinnia

MEDIUM TO EASY IN PLANTABLE POTS: Castor bean, nasturtium, pepper, tomato

DIFFICULT TO GERMINATE IN POTS OR FLATS; USUALLY BEST SOWN DIRECTLY: beans, California poppy, clarkia, corn, impatiens, melon, peas, annual phlox, poppy, vinca (*Catharanthus*)

Resist the urge to let every seedling remain where it sprouts; thin peat pots to one plant each. Thin seeded flats by "pricking and spotting"— "prick" a dotted line around each sprout, then lift it out and "spot" it into a small pot.

GROWING VEGETABLES, FRUITS, AND HERBS

Growing vegetable seedlings in the greenhouse gives you a wider choice of varieties and a jump start on the outdoor gardening season. When those vegetables mature indoors, smiles will spread across your face as you slice tomatoes and cucumbers fresh from the greenhouse and out of season. You can grow many vegetables, herbs, and even fruits in pots, planters, greenhouse beds, growbags, and hydroponic gardens. All demand full sunlight, consistent irrigation, ample fertilizer, supports and trellises for air circulation, and vigilance to control pests. Because most food plants grow best in a moderate temperature range, they are compatible with many other greenhouse plants.

Closely spaced vegetable crops in pots or ground beds can mean more vegetables in a smaller space inside the greenhouse than out in the garden. Such proximity also demands the grower's vigilance to monitor and control pests, and to space plants with mature height in mind so none are shaded.

VEGETABLES AND HERBS

Containers and beds in the greenhouse floor require different care regimes, but both can be used to cultivate food. To get started, try both. Pot perennial herbs and fruits, but build a bed for annual vegetables, herbs, and bedded fruit such as strawberries. Perennial herbs prefer a dry root zone and minimal fertilizer, so plant them in clay pots; use only a slow-release formula every three months. Plant in separate small pots, or combine your favorites. A 10-inch clay pot can hold six shallot bulbs plus an oregano plant and a ground cover of creeping thyme.

Frame up a 1×12-foot bed on the greenhouse floor to grow vegetables and annual herbs such as basil. Grow them in soil mix, with adequate drainage below the bed. If the floor is concrete, add a perforated pipe or slatted bottom or side to allow drainage. Be sure to put aluminum screening over the pipe or slatted opening to keep soil inside. Use the frame to attach trellises; as tomatoes and cucumbers grow up, use the space below for the rest of the salad.

You can grow annual herbs and vegetables directly on a concrete floor using bagged growing mix sold for that purpose ("growbags"). You cut a hole and plant into the bag; there is no dirt on the floor and no bed to dig. However, root space is limited, and the mix heats up rapidly on warm days and may be hard to keep watered. Usually these bags are depleted after one season.

GREENHOUSE FRUITS

The first greenhouses were known as "orangeries," built to protect tropical fruits in temperate climes. Today citrus trees hold the same allure for greenhouse growers: unsurpassed fragrance and delicious fruit. Although citrus requires a warm house, many other fruits need only a cool environment.

Most fruit trees can stay in the same pot for years; your care regime and annual pruning keep them productive. Dwarf varieties are especially well-suited for greenhouses, but pots can help contain the rampant nature of figs and loquat. Build a bed for grapes and strawberries, but plant apples, pears, and stone fruits in pots for summer portability. Consider pollination carefully; self-fertile varieties and trees grafted with several compatible budwoods are a smart investment. Hand pollination, where you play honeybee to the plants, can be an important skill to develop.

GREENHOUSE HYDROPONICS

Hydroponics has been popular indoors and out for decades. Sometimes known as aquaculture, nutriculture, or hydroculture, growing plants without soil has definite advantages. At its best, a hydroponic bed grows plants a bit faster and with lusher leaves than their soil-grown counterparts; it conserves water, fertilizer, and space. Perhaps the biggest advantage to using hydroponics in the greenhouse is that you can grow vegetables without digging a garden bed in the floor or hauling in dirt.

When you place a cutting in a jar of water with fertilizer in it on the kitchen windowsill, or grow an African violet in a reservoir pot, you embark on passive hydroponics. Elementary to set up and maintain, passive hydroponics uses wicks and reservoirs to move the nutrient-filled water into the root zone of the plants. There are no moving parts to maintain, but you must remember to add to the solution regularly.

In active systems, a water solution rich with nutrients is washed or pumped through clay pebbles or other medium that anchors the plants and retains the solution. The most popular examples of active hydroponic systems are the flood-and-drain, top-feed, and NFT, or nutrient-film technique. They all use a reservoir and pump to move the nutrient solution in and out of the root zone to nourish the plants and exchange the air in the growing medium. Flood-and-drain systems are most commonly used by home gardeners.

BUILDING A BASIC BED

Although complete hydroponic kits are available, some systems can be difficult to configure exactly for efficient operation. You can easily build and maintain a classic flood-and-drain hydroponic growing bed with the plan suggested here.

First you need a box to hold the growing medium and plants. You can build the wooden bed shown below or use a sturdy plastic one of similar size. As the drawing illustrates, the bed must be reinforced and lined, with holes in the bottom to accommodate pipes; seal these tightly.

Next set up a perforated pipe about 6 inches long and protected from the growing medium by a sump of wire mesh. The sump lets you clean the holes in the pipe periodically without digging it up. It is advisable to add an overflow pipe at the lower end. Run the pipe through a hole next to the drain, and make the top of it flush with the top of the medium. Either tie it into the drainpipe, or run it directly back to the sump. Place a block under one end of the box to tilt the growing box toward the drain.

Place the hydroponic bed on the greenhouse bench with the reservoir on the floor beneath it. You will need a plastic container (such as a covered garbage can), a submersible pump, and a timer that sits outside the reservoir. Connect the pump to the timer, and set the timer to flood the box twice a day. Be sure the box fills to the top and drains in about 15 minutes.

Hydroponic growing media tend to change as one material proves to be more successful than its predecessors. Pea gravel and rock wool have given way to expanded shale pellets, which drain freely and are lightweight and completely reusable. Any media and every system should be sterilized once a year to promote clean growing conditions.

PLANTS FOR HYDROPONICS

When most people think of hydroponics, they see racks of lettuce or tomatoes climbing high above the shallow growing bed. Both are ideal hydroponic candidates, especially in a winter greenhouse, but more options abound. Try herbs for cooking and aromatherapy, sprouts for salads such as alfalfa and radish, and broccoli, spinach, peas, and annual flowers.

Regular sanitation regimes play a huge role in successful hydroponic gardening. Keep filters and tubing clear; to prevent contamination, be sure soil doesn't spill over into the reservoir.

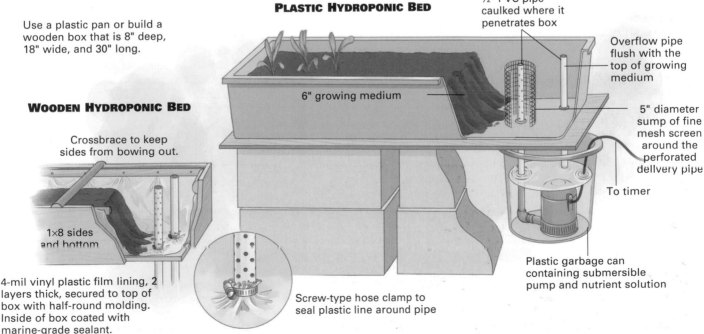

PLASTIC HYDROPONIC BED

½" PVC pipe caulked where it penetrates box

Overflow pipe flush with the top of growing medium

6" growing medium

5" diameter sump of fine mesh screen around the perforated delivery pipe

To timer

Plastic garbage can containing submersible pump and nutrient solution

Use a plastic pan or build a wooden box that is 8" deep, 18" wide, and 30" long.

WOODEN HYDROPONIC BED

Crossbrace to keep sides from bowing out.

1×8 sides and bottom

4-mil vinyl plastic film lining, 2 layers thick, secured to top of box with half-round molding. Inside of box coated with marine-grade sealant.

Screw-type hose clamp to seal plastic line around pipe

PLANT GROUPS FOR GREENHOUSE GROWING

Whether you collect a specific group of plants or simply want to care for the assortment you have, this information will be of value. Each popular greenhouse plant group has its needs and challenges, and knowing which group needs what leads to the best care, maintenance, and propagation.

Crotons delight with shiny leaves painted like organic abstracts in wild shades of red, yellow, and green. These heat lovers and other high-light tropicals drop leaves quickly if overwatered; clay pots are preferred. Stick a finger into the soil to test before watering; when it's dry to your first knuckle, water well, then let dry out again.

LOW-LIGHT HOUSEPLANTS

Under shelves and benches, behind tall plants that face the sun, and in limited-light greenhouses, a host of traditional foliage plants can thrive. This is the group that usually survives inside your house, but they are truly spectacular grown in the greenhouse. Weeping fig holds its leaves, and pothos trails forever. Philodendrons soar up a pole, sprouting bigger leaves the higher they go.

LOOK FOR: *Dieffenbachia* (dumb cane), *Dracaena* (corn plant), *Aglaonema* (Chinese evergreen).

NATIVE TO: Tropical zones worldwide.

FAVORITE FEATURE: Dramatic leaves.

GH CONDITIONS: Moderate to warm temperature range, moderate light.

CULTURE NOTES: Grow in premium soil mix. Let soil surface barely dry out before watering. Apply water-soluble fertilizer twice a month in spring and summer, timed-release fertilizer in fall and once in winter.

PROPAGATE BY: Cuttings, air layering, division.

CHALLENGES: Mealybugs, overwatering.

HIGH-LIGHT HOUSEPLANTS

Tropical plants grown for their gorgeous flowers and bold leaves can tolerate low-light conditions but come into their own in a bright, humid environment. Some demand high humidity; *Anthurium, Croton,* and *Aphelandra* (zebra plant), for example, fade fast in the temperate zone unless they're in a greenhouse, where their brightly painted and striped leaves can be yours.

LOOK FOR: *Saintpaulia* (African violet), *Sinningia, Ananas* (variegated pineapple).

NATIVE TO: Tropical zones worldwide.

FAVORITE FEATURE: Flowers and leaves.

GH CONDITIONS: Warm range only, high light to full sun.

CULTURE NOTES: Grow in premium soil mix. Allow to dry between waterings. Provide water-soluble fertilizer weekly through spring and summer, and pelleted, timed-release fertilizer once in fall and once in winter.

PROPAGATE BY: Cuttings, leaves, offsets.

CHALLENGES: Low light and overwatering.

Move low-light plants such as this dwarf Schefflera arboricola 'Variegata' up one pot size annually and they'll grow larger each year.

ORCHIDS

Close your eyes, and see yourself in the greenhouse. It's comfortable inside, although north winds howl outside around bare trees. If you see only one plant family, it could be orchids. With their wide range of flower sizes, colors, and plant forms, they make a fascinating collection. Some varieties are demanding, but most like what you like: warm days, cool nights, and moderate relative humidity.

LOOK FOR: Dwarf *Cymbidium*, *Dendrobium*, *Odontoglossum* (including tiger orchid), *Phalaenopsis* (moth orchid).

NATIVE TO: 20,000 species grow around the world in tropical and temperate zones.

FAVORITE FEATURE: Flowers.

GH CONDITIONS: Cool to moderate temperature range, bright light.

CULTURE NOTES: Grow in orchid bark mix and water twice weekly. Let pots dry out and rest between flowering cycles. Apply water-soluble fertilizer monthly in spring and summer, timed-release fertilizer in fall and winter and whenever plants are repotted.

PROPAGATE BY: Division, offsets, seeds.

CHALLENGES: Bright light but little direct sun, needs perfect drainage.

CACTI AND SUCCULENTS

For a small greenhouse space and a warm, dry interior environment, nothing beats cacti and succulents as a focal point for collecting plants. You can fit many mature specimens from this group into limited bench space. In nature these plants adapt to a waterless environment; interesting leaves and bizarre flowers are your reward for cultivating the science fiction characters of the plant world.

LOOK FOR: *Aloe vera*, *Mammillaria* (pincushion cactus), *Sedum* (including donkey's tail and rosary vine), *Hylocereus* (night-blooming cereus), *Cephalocereus* (old man cactus).

NATIVE TO: Arid regions worldwide, including Mexico and South Africa.

FAVORITE FEATURE: Unusual forms, water-storing leaves.

GH CONDITIONS: Moderate to warm temperature range, low humidity, full sun.

CULTURE NOTES: Grow in cactus potting mix and water only when dry. Apply timed-release fertilizer two times a year, and dilute water-soluble fertilizer during bloom season.

PROPAGATE BY: Offsets, cuttings.

CHALLENGES: Overwatering, low light, leaf spots.

Named for the insects their flowers can resemble, moth orchids (Phalaenopsis and Doritaenopsis) thrive in warm nights with ample humidity. To encourage rebloom of moth orchids, cut back the spent flower spike to the second or third node (swelling) in one stem.

Terra-cotta pots, made of porous clay, allow water to evaporate quickly through their surfaces and away from the root zones of plants, making them ideal for cacti and succulents. Big containers can hold attractive mixed collections. Buy pots with holes cut in the bottom and unglazed surfaces to promote drainage and evaporation.

PLANT GROUPS FOR GREENHOUSE GROWING
continued

Plant only one color or kind of bulb in each pot for best effect, then display the finished pots together.

FLOWERING PLANTS

You can grow flowering plants in the greenhouse that cannot survive the conditions outside. Container gardening in the greenhouse give you control of the elements, so you can be bold in making plant choices, growing one of this and one of that to your endless pleasure.

LOOK FOR: *Pelargonium* (including ivy geranium), *Primula* (primrose), *Passiflora* (passionflower).

NATIVE TO: High-light temperate zones.

FAVORITE FEATURE: Flowers, trailing habit.

GH CONDITIONS: Cool to moderate temperature range, full sun.

CULTURE NOTES: Grow in a premium potting mix. Let soil dry out between waterings, but do not let plants wilt. Apply timed-release fertilizer at potting, then water-soluble fertilizer monthly.

PROPAGATE BY: Seeds, cuttings.

CHALLENGES: Whitefly and other piercing and sucking insects. Low light makes plants susceptible to disease.

Root or buy four small ivy geraniums to plant a 10-inch hanging basket. Use a balanced soluble fertilizer (20-20-20) until leaves fill the basket, then switch to a formula with a higher middle number (phosphorus) to encourage flowering.

FLOWERING BULBS

The bulbs that appear so briefly in the garden each year know no season in the greenhouse. The tulips you plant today bloom in a few weeks, the amaryllis thrill throughout the fall, and the freesias scent the place through the depths of the hardest winter. Bed-grown gladiolas never get beaten by rainstorms, and successive planting delivers the blooms right on your timetable.

LOOK FOR: *Clivia, Freesia, Hyacinthus, Hippeastrum* (amaryllis).

NATIVE TO: Temperate zones primarily.

FAVORITE FEATURE: Flowers and fragrance.

GH CONDITIONS: Cool to moderate temperature range, full sun.

CULTURE NOTES: Plant in a well-drained premium potting mix; water at potting, then only when dry. Fertilize only at potting. If leaves emerge pale, apply a water-soluble fertilizer.

PROPAGATE BY: New bulbs, offsets.

CHALLENGES: Too much heat causes stems to stretch and flowers to drop.

SHOWY TROPICALS TO OVERWINTER

Probably no other greenhouse project impresses the neighbors as much as the blooming tropical plants you return to the patio early each spring. After a winter of tender care, the pots of fragrant jasmine and bright hibiscus and bougainvillea brim with color and renewed life. When summer ends, the plants go back in the greenhouse. With a little care, they bloom for Thanksgiving, too.

LOOK FOR: *Hibiscus, Bougainvillea, Mandevilla, Jasminum*.

NATIVE TO: High-light tropical regions.

FAVORITE FEATURE: Flowers.

GH CONDITIONS: Cool to moderate temperature range, bright light only.

CULTURE NOTES: Apply timed-release fertilizer in early spring and midsummer, water-soluble fertilizer monthly March through July. Hold flowering tropicals in a resting state through winter in a cool house. Give minimal water and only a slow-release fertilizer applied once in fall. Or encourage flowering and active growth with more warmth and soluble fertilizer applied monthly.

PROPAGATE BY: Cuttings.

CHALLENGES: Leaf drop, whiteflies, and other piercing and sucking insects.

BROMELIADS

The first one delights you, and the search for more of this interesting group begins. The trail leads to tall vase shapes, flat spirals, spiky flowers, and tiny clusters deep in the well.

LOOK FOR: *Tillandsia, Guzmania, Billbergia*.

NATIVE TO: North, Central, and South America.

FAVORITE FEATURE: Leaves and flowers.

GH CONDITIONS: Moderate to warm temperature range, bright but diffused light.

CULTURE NOTES: Grow terrestrials in a well-drained premium potting mix or an orchid mix, and epiphytes on boards covered with sphagnum moss. Water weekly and keep water in the flower cup. Apply fertilizer to the soil only (not in the cup)—either timed-release fertilizer in spring and fall, or water-soluble fertilizer (half strength) in spring and summer.

PROPAGATE BY: Offsets.

CHALLENGES: This is a big family whose species have different needs.

Maintain heat-loving tropicals over winter in semidormancy with minimal light, water, and fertilizer. Or, if space permits, grow them on the bench with ample amounts of light, water, and fertilizer for midwinter flowers.

Fill the flowering cup of these bromeliads with water, and apply fertilizer directly to the soil when you irrigate. After blooming, the mother plant declines and offsets appear at the base that you can divide and pot.

PLANT GROUPS FOR GREENHOUSE GROWING
continued

Press tiny seeds for bedding plants into sterile seedling soil mix, then sprinkle on more just to cover. A board or another flat on top of the seed flat will keep moisture in and promote faster sprouting. Remove the cover immediately when seeds sprout.

GREENHOUSE CUT FLOWERS

What could be a more satisfying result of building a greenhouse than a vase full of cut flowers you have grown there? Bulbs and a host of stiff-stemmed flowers grow well in greenhouse floor beds. Whether it's a dinner party in January or a June wedding, the flowers you grow yourself make the event. Press a few of your first blooms for posterity, and be justifiably proud.

LOOK FOR: *Gladiolus, Gerbera, Antirrhinum* (snapdragon), *Dianthus* (carnation).

NATIVE TO: Temperate zones.

FAVORITE FEATURE: Showy flowers on sturdy stems.

GH CONDITIONS: Moderate temperature range, full sun.

CULTURE NOTES: Grow in a premium potting mix, and water to keep soil just moist. Apply water-soluble fertilizer weekly through growing season.

PROPAGATE BY: Seeds, cuttings, new bulbs.

CHALLENGES: Overwatering and crowded conditions promote disease; flowers need support as they grow.

BEDDING PLANTS

Garden centers erupt with annual flowers and vegetables each spring, but there are more seeds to choose from than transplants, in a rainbow of colors with different habits to make your garden stand out. Uncommon varieties (old or new) may be available only as seeds.

LOOK FOR: Double-flowered impatiens, Prince's feather celosia, heirloom tomatoes.

NATIVE TO: Temperate and subtropical zones.

FAVORITE FEATURE: Unusual flower colors and forms, dwarf and heirloom vegetables.

GH CONDITIONS: Warm environment to germinate, then moderate temperatures with ventilation to maintain moderate humidity. Harden off in cool house or outdoors before transplanting.

CULTURE NOTES: Buy fresh seed and use sterile potting mix in clean containers. Seed sparingly in individual plastic cells, and thin to one seedling per cell when true leaves appear. Water from below whenever possible, and fertilize weekly.

PROPAGATE BY: Seeds.

CHALLENGES: Damping-off, stretching due to crowding or low light.

Grow a few flowers for cutting in pots. Or, as with these gerberas, line them out in beds to use growing space most efficiently.

WOODY PLANTS

Once you have rooted fleshy cuttings and started seeds, the propagation bug has bitten and woody plants will tempt you. The coolest part of the winter greenhouse—perhaps the floor farthest from the heater—may not have another use in your initial management plan. But it makes an ideal spot to place a flat of spirea or forsythia, or to care for your potted azaleas and gardenias.

LOOK FOR: *Chaenomeles*, *Salix* (pussy willow), *Hydrangea*.

NATIVE TO: Temperate zones worldwide.

FAVORITE FEATURE: Form, flowers.

GH CONDITIONS: Cool temperature range, moderate light for rooting, bright light for flowering.

CULTURE NOTES: Grow in an all-purpose premium potting mix and water sparingly. Apply timed-release fertilizer at potting and once a year thereafter.

PROPAGATE BY: Hardwood cuttings.

CHALLENGES: Maintaining proper temperature and moisture.

WATER-GARDEN PLANTS

The beauty of a water garden fills the summer air with soothing sounds, lovely flowers, and endlessly amusing fish. For most pond gardeners, cold weather brings the off-season, and those plants that cannot overwinter outdoors must be protected. You can hold tender water plants in the greenhouse, or set up a minipond to keep them growing.

LOOK FOR: *Nymphaea* 'Dauben', 'Charles Thomas', 'Hilary', and *N. colorata* are day bloomers. *N.* 'Missouri' and 'Red Flare' are night bloomers.

NATIVE TO: Tropical regions.

FAVORITE FEATURE: Flowers, fragrance.

GH CONDITIONS: Cool to moderate temperature range, bright light.

CULTURE NOTES: Lift the containers out of the pond before frost and cut back the leaves. Put them in a child's pool or other small pond inside the greenhouse, and look for a few small flowers before spring. When annuals can be safely transplanted outdoors, pot the water lilies in fresh soil containing fertilizer and return them to the outdoor water garden.

PROPAGATE BY: Some water lilies produce "vivips," little plants at the center of mature leaves. Once the babies are big enough to handle, cut them off and press them into shallow pots with soil, then barely submerge the pots in the pond. Lower them as they grow to keep stems long.

CHALLENGES: Water temperatures below 60 degrees F, especially in the absence of sunlight, can rot lilies.

To encourage woody plants to rebloom in containers, prune lightly after flowering. When roots fill the pot, prune both tops and roots to maintain their balance, then repot with fresh soil in the same container.

Make space on a bright bench for tropical pond plants, and watch for new babies to lift and propagate. Low light and moderate temperatures will keep even tender lilies alive over winter.

MASTER PROJECTS

Greenhouse growing brings rewards every day: seeds sprout, flowers bloom out of season, you make cuttings and one plant becomes three. Every year you think of something else to grow, and you experiment with soils and pots. Use these ideas to launch your own master projects in the greenhouse.

Pot tulips with the pointed end up, cover with 2 inches of soil, and keep cool until sprouts appear.

Air layering a Schefflera

FORCING BULBS

To bring bulbs such as Dutch iris, tulips, and paperwhites into bloom when you want them can be a poetic gardening experience. Each bulb holds its flowers locked inside, awaiting the turn of your greenhouse key.

To have pots of narcissus just about to bloom in early December, buy bulbs as soon as possible in fall. Classic 'Paper White' or golden 'Soleil d'Or' make excellent pot plants. Put the bulbs in the crisper drawer of your refrigerator until November 1. Pot narcissus in marble chips or 1-inch gravel; place the bulbs so their big bottoms are covered but the sloped sides (the "shoulders") and growing point stand above. You can use any pot, but know that narcissus are top-heavy in flower. Sturdy crockery pots with no drain hole make excellent containers. One about 6 inches across and 3 to 4 inches deep holds seven to nine bulbs. Water once after planting. To keep stems from stretching, put the potted bulbs in a cool, dark place until they have 4 inches of white stem showing. Then move them to a sunny bench and water weekly until you put on the gift ribbons.

Buy Dutch iris bulbs along with your narcissus to grow cut flowers; any color will do, but 'Wedgewood' remains the best blue performer. The blooms last about five days each, so this project calls for staggered planting to prolong your pleasure with no more real work. Plant iris in a planter box with a layer of gravel at least 4 inches deep topped with 4 to 6 inches of an all-purpose potting mix. Each iris needs a 3×5-inch space, so a box 15×20 inches will hold 20 bulbs to start. Plant in a grid pattern with the tip of each bulb level with the top of the mix after watering. Put the box in a cold spot until the plants are 2 inches tall, then move to a sunny bench to flower. After seven weeks, plant another crop of bulbs between the rows in the box. In about 12 weeks, you'll be cutting the first flowers. After 13 weeks, plant a bulb next to each of the first bulbs you planted for yet more iris.

AIR LAYERING

Sphagnum moss does more than line hanging baskets. You use it in the greenhouse to grow and propagate plants. This organic material creates a perfect environment for roots that thrive on lots of moisture with excellent drainage and air circulation. Many tropical houseplants need just this combination.

Air layering happens naturally in the rain forest when a stem splits, some organic matter lands on it, and a new shoot emerges in the humid climate. You must rehydrate sphagnum moss, which is dried when packaged for sale, before using it to air layer or line wire baskets. Tear off two fistfuls of moss and put in a bucket of water for an hour. Stir to be sure it's wet, then squeeze out the water and rewet the moss several times. Squeeze out most of the last dunking, and you're ready to go.

Any mature plant with a fleshy stem makes a good candidate, such as *Ficus, Schefflera,* or *Dracaena.* All these plants tend to get spindly with age, growing bare stems with tufts of leaves at their top. Select a spot on a stem about 10 inches below the healthy growth and cut a diagonal slice across the stem. Put a piece of a toothpick in the slit to hold it open. Fashion a lump of wet sphagnum moss around the whole stem, including the slit; make it 4 to 6 inches long and 2 inches or so deep. Cover completely with clear plastic film secured above and below. Use 4- or 6-mil greenhouse film, or substitute a double layer of food wrap. Plastic-coated twist ties from your kitchen work well to hold the plastic film in place. You can purchase a roll of plastic film at a garden center.

Keep the plant out of direct sun, and water it as usual. Look for white roots visible in the plastic after a few months; when you're satisfied there are enough, cut the stem below the root ball, remove the wrap, and pot the rooted growth.

LAYERING AND GRAFTING

Layering and grafting used to be the only way to propagate cultivars of woody plants. Both techniques can be mastered with practice.

Layering, performed in late fall, uses the mother plant to sustain the new baby. Any woody plant that grows long, supple stems and loses its leaves (such as grape, trailing roses, and forsythia) will root from layers. Put a flat of soil mix near the mother's container and bend a stem toward it. Lay the stem in the flat with 1 foot of its tip exposed. Cover the stem in the flat with more soil, and put a block or brick on top of the soil to hold down the stem. You'll know it has rooted when the tip leafs out along with the mother plant. Cut it off behind the layer and pot it.

Grafting and its companion, budding, put a stem cutting (the scion) from one plant together with the rootstock of another to form a new plant. Grafts—whip, cleft, bark, and others—depend on a careful matching of the cambium layers (the plant tissue just under the bark) to succeed. T-budding puts the new growing point inside the stock bark—clean cuts and a tight fit make for a healthy union. Grafting demands a very sharp knife and steady hand. Practice cutting buds and joining scions, then make several grafts to be sure one will take.

Purchase bud wood or collect budded scion wood from the middle of stems in late fall or very early spring. Mark the top of the scion, then store cold in damp sawdust until the stock plants are in vigorous spring growth— that is, when the bark slips off easily. Match the bottom of the scion to the top of the rootstock, strip off any bark in the way, and join them quickly. Protect from the air with nursery tape, or grafting bands and grafting wax. Allow several weeks for the wounds to heal and callus to form; replace the seal if it cracks. For insurance, make a few more grafts than you want, because not all may take.

Likely candidates for grafting and budding are close relatives, either within a species or a genus. Grafting desirable scion woods onto dwarf rootstocks allows greenhouse growers to produce full-size fruit and flowers on smaller plants more suited to greenhouse space.

REBLOOMING HOLIDAY PLANTS

When your Christmas cactus finishes blooming in late winter, give it a rest. Pick off the old flowers, drastically reduce watering, and set the pot aside in low light for two months. Then add a timed-released fertilizer, and water only when dry until September. Fertilize once and increase watering. As nights get longer (12 hours in most regions by late September), and if you allow no additional light, flowers will develop in nine to 12 weeks.

Once a pot mum has spent its blooms, cut back each flowering stem to green growth, or about 4 inches tall. Slip the root ball out of the pot to examine it. If root-bound, make a cut straight down each side of the ball and replant in a slightly larger pot with new soil. Provide regular water and fertilizer until the plant doubles in size, then pinch off half the new growth. Continue watering and fertilizing. The plant will bloom on its own eventually, or you can force it with the black cloth treatment. When the plant is about 10 inches tall, initiate flowering by providing 11 hours of darkness each day. Put up a black cloth drape or other device to exclude light, and use it religiously to extend the night's length. Once the buds have formed and swelled, stop covering at night. You can do this any time of year that you can provide 60-degree nights and daytime temperatures no higher than 85 degrees F. How long it takes depends on the variety and conditions, but generally, for Mother's Day blooms in early May, you need to have plants ready for long nights by early February.

Poinsettias respond to the same general regime: Cut off old flowering stems in February, grow the plant with adequate water and fertilizer, repot if needed, pinch at least twice over the summer to keep growth compact, and grow until it develops red bracts naturally around January. For Christmas blooming, begin the black cloth treatment on September 1.

A cautionary note about all black cloth projects: Any light source, including sunlight and streetlights, whether direct or reflected, can disrupt the cycle. Cover the pots completely, without the cloth touching the plants. Do not let heat build up, and remove the cloth on schedule every day. Water and fertilize regularly. Although naturally long nights will produce flowers, this special treatment can lead to earlier blooms at holiday time.

To create a T-bud graft, open a T in the bark and insert a shield-shaped bud with one growing eye. Like all grafts, the T-bud graft attaches to its stock to become one plant.

Holiday cactus leaves shrivel with exhaustion after blooming, but you can rejuvenate them for another season after two months' rest.

RESOURCES

ORGANIZATIONS:

Hobby Greenhouse Association
8 Glen Terrace
Bedford MA 01730-2048
781-275-0377
www.hobbygreenhouse.org

Cooperative Extension Services, by
state: www.farmboys.com/resources
/ext_serv/ext_serv.htm

NATIONAL CATALOG COMPANIES FOR GREENHOUSE KITS AND SUPPLIES:

Charley's Greenhouses and Garden
    Supplies
17979 State Route 536
Mount Vernon WA 98273-3269
800-322-4707
www.charleysgreenhouse.com

Gardener's Supply Company
128 Intervale Road
Burlington VT 05401
888-833-1412
www.gardeners.com

HOBBY GREENHOUSE MANUFACTURERS:

Carolina Greenhouses
1504 Cunningham Road
Kinston NC 28501
252-523-9300
www.carolinagreenhouses.com

Crop King Greenhouses
5050 Greenwich Road
Seville OH 44273
330-769-2002
www.cropking.com

Florian Greenhouse, Inc.
549 Aviation Boulevard
Georgetown SC 29440
800-356-7426
www.florian-greenhouse.com

Gothic Arch Greenhouses, Inc.
P.O. Box 1564–OR
Mobile AL 36633-1564
800-531-4769
www.GothicArchGreenhouses.com

Grow-it Greenhouses
17 Wood Street
West Haven CT 06516
800-435-6601
www.growitgreenhouses.com

Hobby Gardens Greenhouses
P.O. Box 193
New London NH 03257
603-927-4283
www.hobbygardens.com

Hoop House Greenhouse Kits
Rt 28
South Yarmouth MA 02664
800-760-5192
www.hoophouse.com

Janco Greenhouses
9390 Davis Avenue
Laurel MD 20723-1993
800-323-6933
www.jancoinc.com

Santa Barbara Greenhouses
721 Richmond Avenue
Oxnard CA 93030
800-544-5276
www.sbgreenhouse.com

Sturdi-Built Greenhouse Mfg. Co.
11304 SW Boones Ferry Road
Portland OR 97219
800-334-4115
www.sturdi-built.com

Sunglo Greenhouses
214 21st Street SE
Auburn WA 98002
253-833-4529
www.sunglogreenhouses.com

Texas Greenhouse Company
2524 White Settlement Road
Fort Worth TX 76107
800-227-5447
www.texasgreenhouse.com

Turner Greenhouses
1500 US Highway 117S
Goldsboro NC 27533
919-734-8345
www.turnergreenhouses.com

SPECIALIZED EQUIPMENT MANUFACTURERS:

Batrow Inc.
171 Short Beach Road
Short Beach CT 06405
203-488-2578
e-mail: batrow@aol.com
(Single- and multi-station controllers)

Continental Products Company
1150 East 222 Street
Euclid OH 44117
216-531-0710
www.continentalprod.com
(Shading compound)

Hydro-gardens, Inc.
P.O. Box 25845
Colorado Springs CO 80936-5845
800-634-6362
www.hydro-gardens.com
(Hydroponic equipment and supplies)

Rough Brothers
5513 Vine Street
Cincinnati OH 45217
www.roughbros.com
513-242-0310
(Greenhouse replacement parts)

SolarSun, Inc.
15 Blueberry Ridge Road
Setauket NY 11733
877-276-5277
www.solsun.com
(Condensate and shade control
    coatings)

Southern Burner Corporation
P.O. Box 885
Chickasha OK 73023
405-224-5000
www. southernburner.com
(Non-electric heaters)

Thermalarm Products, Inc.
P.O. Box 809, Route 153 South
Center Ossipee NH 03814
603-539-3444
www.thermalarm.com
(Temperature alarm systems)

USDA PLANT HARDINESS ZONE MAP

This map of climate zones helps you select plants for your garden that will survive a typical winter in your region. The United States Department of Agriculture (USDA) developed the map, basing the zones on the lowest recorded temperatures across North America. Zone 1 is the coldest area and Zone 11 is the warmest.

Plants are classified by the coldest temperature and zone they can endure. For example, plants hardy to Zone 6 survive where winter temperatures drop to –10° F. Those hardy to Zone 8 die long before it's that cold. These plants may grow in colder regions but must be replaced each year. Plants rated for a range of hardiness zones can usually survive winter in the coldest region as well as tolerate the summer heat of the warmest one.

To find your hardiness zone, note the approximate location of your community on the map, then match the color band marking that area to the key.

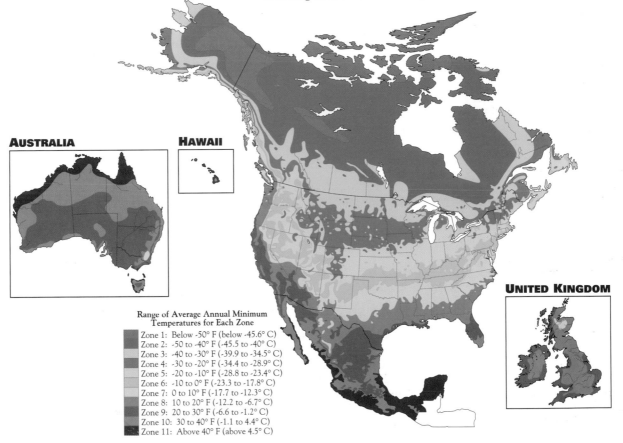

AUSTRALIA

HAWAII

UNITED KINGDOM

Range of Average Annual Minimum Temperatures for Each Zone

Zone 1: Below -50° F (below -45.6° C)
Zone 2: -50 to -40° F (-45.5 to -40° C)
Zone 3: -40 to -30° F (-39.9 to -34.5° C)
Zone 4: -30 to -20° F (-34.4 to -28.9° C)
Zone 5: -20 to -10° F (-28.8 to -23.4° C)
Zone 6: -10 to 0° F (-23.3 to -17.8° C)
Zone 7: 0 to 10° F (-17.7 to -12.3° C)
Zone 8: 10 to 20° F (-12.2 to -6.7° C)
Zone 9: 20 to 30° F (-6.6 to -1.2° C)
Zone 10: 30 to 40° F (-1.1 to 4.4° C)
Zone 11: Above 40° F (above 4.5° C)

METRIC CONVERSIONS

U.S. Units to Metric Equivalents			Metric Units to U.S. Equivalents		
To Convert From	**Multiply By**	**To Get**	**To Convert From**	**Multiply By**	**To Get**
Inches	25.4	Millimeters	Millimeters	0.0394	Inches
Inches	2.54	Centimeters	Centimeters	0.3937	Inches
Feet	30.48	Centimeters	Centimeters	0.0328	Feet
Feet	0.3048	Meters	Meters	3.2808	Feet
Yards	0.9144	Meters	Meters	1.0936	Yards

To convert from degrees Fahrenheit (F) to degrees Celsius (C), first subtract 32, then multiply by $\frac{5}{9}$.

To convert from degrees Celsius to degrees Fahrenheit, multiply by $\frac{9}{5}$, then add 32.

INDEX

Page numbers in **boldface type** indicate a photograph or illustration.

3118